T5-DGI-324

YOUR LUCKY NUMBERS ... FOREVER!

by
Anna Riva

Author of

Prayer Book
Candle Burning Magic
Powers of the Psalms
Devotions to the Saints
Secrets of Magical Seals
Modern Herbal Spellbook
Modern Witchcraft Spellbook
Golden Secrets of Mystic Oils
Magic with Incense and Powders
Spellcraft, Hexcraft & Witchcraft
Voodoo Handbook of Cult Secrets

INTERNATIONAL IMPORTS
236 W. MANCHESTER AVE.
LOS ANGELES, CA 90003

Copyright © 1992
ISBN 0-943832-17-9

NOTICE: All rights reserved. No part of this book may be reproduced in any form without prior permission of the publisher. No claims of supernatural effects or powers are made for any item mentioned herein, and the material is strictly legendary.

CONTENTS

NOTE: Throughout the number charts in this book, Zeros have been included in their natural order, and can be used if they are appropriate. If Zeros are not pertinent, drop them and replace them with your own Personal Number.

HOURLY NUMBERS

12 to 1 o'clock 1		6 to 7 o'clock 7	
1 to 2 o'clock 2		7 to 8 o'clock 8	
2 to 3 o'clock 3		8 to 9 o'clock 9	
3 to 4 o'clock 4		9 to 10 o'clock 1	
4 to 5 o'clock 5		10 to 11 o'clock 2	
5 to 6 o'clock 6		11 to 12 o'clock 3	

There is little attention given to the favorable or unfavorable influences of time except that, should your daily number be in harmony with the hour's number, your activity during that time will probably result in pleasure, monetary gain, spiritual enrichment, or other advantageous effects. This applies whether the project is conducted in the AM or PM hours.

A

HOW TO FIND ONE'S BIRTH NUMBER

Many believers in the power of numbers feel that the date of one's arrival into this world is of more importance than the name one is given by others. The belief is based on the fact that, during a lifetime, the name can change -- sometimes several times -- but the birthdate endures always and forever the same.

It is quite simple to figure the birth number. It consists of the month's number *(1 through 12),* the day's number *(1 through 31)* and the year's number *(a total of the four digits).*

MONTHS		MONTHS	
January	1	July	7
February	2	August	8
March	3	September	9
April	4	October	10
May	5	November	11
June	6	December	12

As an example, let's determine the birth number of one born on August 6, 1954.

(Month)	August	8
(Day)	6	6
(Year)	1954 $(1+9+5+4)$	19
	Total	33

Then 3 plus 3 totals 6 which is the Birth Number for that birthdate.

Or, for one born on January 20, 1922, the birth number is determined to be as illustrated below.

(Month	January	1
(Day)	20	2
(Year)	1922 $(1+9+2+2)$	14
	Total	17

Finally, 1 plus 7 totals 8 which is the Birth Number.

HOW TO FIND
ONE'S NAME NUMBER

It is quite easy to determine anyone's Name Number. All you need is the complete name. Whether the birth name, one acquired by marriage or other legal change, or an assumed one as used is a personal choice.

Generally, the modern alphabet we are all familiar with is chosen. However, for those who wish to use the Chaldean which dates back to 1,000 BC, this is also given.

1	2	3	4	5	6	7	8	9	MODERN
A	B	C	D	E	F	G	H	I	
J	K	L	M	N	O	P	Q	R	
S	T	U	V	W	X	Y	Z		

1	2	3	4	5	6	7	8	CHALDEAN
A	B	C	D	E	U	O	F	
I	K	G	M	H	V	Z	P	
J	R	L	T	N	W			
Q		S	X					
Y								

The sacred number 9 is omitted in the Chaldean alphabet but, of course, it is included in totaling the letter values.

Zeros have no value in numerology and are eliminated from totals. For instance, should the addition of the name numbers result in a total of 60, the zero is dropped and the Name Number is Six.

Where a total might be 64, the 6 + 4 becomes 10, and the zero is eliminated, leaving the Name Number as One.

As an example, let's use the author's name with the modern alphabet.

```
A   N   N   A     R   E   B   E   C   C   A     R   I   V   A
1   5   5   1     9   5   2   5   3   3   1     9   9   4   1
```

We now add all numbers to a total:

$1+5+5+1+9+5+2+5+3+3+1+9+9+4+1 = 63$

Then add $6 + 3 = 9$ which is the Name Number.

By using the Chaldean alphabet, the result is sometimes different.

```
A   N   N   A     R   E   B   E   C   C   A     R   I   V   A
1   5   5   1     2   5   2   5   3   3   1     2   1   6   1
```

Add $1+5+5+1+2+5+2+5+3+3+1+2+1+6+1 = 43$

Then 4 plus 3 results in 7 as the Name Number.

c

HOW TO FIND
ONE'S ZODIAC NUMBER

Many feel that the astrological sign under which one is born may be significant in one's life and can be included as a consideration when selecting numbers on which you plan to wager, begin a project, start a trip, or make an important decision.

Birth Date Is:	Zodiac Sign	Zodiac Number
January 21 to February 19	Aquarius	4
February 20 to March 20	Pisces	7
March 21 to April 20	Aries	9
April 21 to May 22	Taurus	6
May 23 to June 21	Gemini	5
June 22 to July 22	Cancer	2
July 23 to August 22	Leo	1
August 23 to September 22	Virgo	5
September 23 to October 22	Libra	6
October 23 to November 21	Scorpio	9
November 22 to December 22	Sagittarius	3
December 23 to January 20	Capricorn	8

PLANETARY NUMBERS

Each planet has a particular number with which it is associated as well as specific areas of influence. For those who wish to include planetary influences in their consideration, their number and areas of influence are given.

Planet	Number	Influences
Jupiter	1	Legal and financial matters, religion
Mars	2	Warfare and military personnel, medicine
Mercury	3	Business affairs, communication, travel
Moon	4	Imagination, friendship, intelligence
Neptune	5	Leisure, psychic sciences, the unknown
Saturn	6	Science, government, serenity
Sun	7	Art, knowledge, success, dignity
Uranus	8	Education, discipline, writing
Venus	9	Harmony, beauty, charm, love, pride

Each planet is the ruler of its respective day of the week, in order from Sun on Sunday through Saturn on Saturday.

Sunday . . . . Sun
Monday . . . . Moon
Tuesday . . . . Mars
Wednesday . . . . Mercury
Thursday . . . . Jupiter
Friday . . . . Venus
Saturday . . . . Saturn

Hence, the days are numbered the same as the planet which rules each, as follows:

Sunday 7
Monday 4
Tuesday 2
Wednesday 3
Thursday 1
Friday 9
Saturday 6

E

THE "GOOD"
AND THE "BAD"

Everyone seems to have "good" days or "bad" periods for no apparent reason. It is possible that there are some influences beyond all human control which have a factor in this seeming phenomena.

Those who believe in the power of numbers are convinced that by knowing in advance of these times which may be either favorable or unfavorable gives one an opportunity to offset the negative potential or to enhance the positive aspects of any situation.

The following chart of Lucky and Unlucky Months may help one take advantage of fortunate periods and better cope with the less fortunate times.

If Your Personal Number Is:	Lucky Months
1	March, April, July, August
2	April, May, June, July
3	November, December
4	January, February, July, August
5	May, June, August, September
6	April, May, September, October
7	February, March, June, July
8	January, September, October, December
9	January, March, April, December

	Unlucky Months
1	January, June, December
2	November, December
3	April, May, October
4	June, December
5	January, February, July
6	February, March, August
7	January, August
8	May, June, November
9	February, August, September

Ever wonder why you meet some people and seem to "hit if off" with them right away, while others rub you the wrong way no matter what they do?

It could be that your Personal Number simply is not compatible with theirs, or that your individual numbers blend to complement each other in small ways which brings almost instant affinity.

If Your Personal Number Is:	It Is Harmonious With:	It Is Incompatible With:
1	4, 8	7
2	7, 9	6
3	5, 6, 9	8
4	1, 8	3, 5
5	3	7
6	3, 7, 9	2
7	2, 6	1
8	1, 4	3
9	2, 3, 9	7

NUMBERS AND THE LOTTERY

A majority of states have lotteries, some offering only one or two, while at least ten have three or more.

In the Lotto games, to win the maximum prize, the player must choose five or six selected numbers from a field of from twenty-five in West Virginia to eleven from eighty in Canada.

In the lottery, some states offer both three-digit and four-digit lotteries.

It is quite easy to relate the daily numbers given in this book to the lottery if you wish to use it for this purpose.

As an example, first choice might be the Birth Number since it is considered most effective of all.

Next in importance is the Name Numbers.

Following the above two, check your Astrological or Zodiac Number, and consider including it.

Next inclusion to be considered are the numbers which are most harmonious with your Personal Number. You may decide to exclude those which are incompatible with your Personal Number.

Many will proceed to the Planetary Influences, each affecting certain days of the week.

Sunday	Sun	7
Monday	Moon	4
Tuesday	Mars	2
Wednesday	Mercury	3
Thursday	Jupiter	1
Friday	Neptune & Venus	5 & 9
Saturday	Saturn & Uranus	6 & 8

From the above, you have four digits --- Birth, Name, Astrological, and Planetary. If playing a 4-digit game, the above will fulfill your requirements. For a 3-digit game, choose Birth, Name, and Astrological --- or, if your instincts guide you, pick three of the four with which you feel most confident.

For those contests which require more than the above, refer to "How to Use This Book in Games of Chance" (Chapter 9).

HOW TO USE THIS BOOK
IN GAMES OF CHANCE

From the Numbers and The Lottery page, you have the four personal numbers which are of most significance to you, and these can be used as a basis when making your selection. Whether you choose these or others from your own special system is entirely your individual choice. It is your personal affinity with your numbers and your confidence in them which gives them power.

This book gives you a number for each day in 2, 3, 4, 5, and 6 digits. These can cover most needs, but should a larger than six-digit number be needed, it is suggested that the following method could be used for a selection.

7 digits: use your own one digit Personal Number, and the six digit column given in the book.

8 digits: use the six digit and two digit columns.

9 digits: use the six digit and three digit columns.

10 digits: combine the six digit and four digit columns.

11 digits: select the six digit and the five digit columns.

12 digits use the six digit, the five digit columns, and your Personal Number.

13 digits: combine the six digit, the five digit, and the two digit columns.

14 digits: select the six digit, the five digit, and the three digit columns.

15 digits try the six digit, five digit, and the four digit columns.

16 digits: combine the six digit, five digit, four digit columns, plus your Personal Number

17 digits: use the six digit, five digit, four digit, and two digit columns.

18 digits: use the six digit, five digit, four digit, and three digit columns.

19 digits: use the six digit, five digit, four digit, three digit columns, plus your Personal Number.

20 digits: use the six digit, five digit, four digit, three digit, plus two digit columns.

And so forth.

Note: Throughout the number charts in this book, Zeros have been included in their natural order, and can be used if they are appropriate. If Zeros are not pertinent, drop them and replace them with your own Personal Numbers.

COMPATIBLE COLORS

Particular colors seem to be more soothing, uplifting, and exhilarating for certain persons, while other colors may bring disheartening feelings and melancholy.

The list given includes the colors which reputedly are most strengthening and enhancing to the various Personal Numbers.

1   Cream, Gold, Green, Orange, White, Yellow

2   Blue, Gray, Green, White, Yellow

3   Azure, Blue, Mauve, Pink, Purple, Violet

4   Blue, Gold, Gray, Orange, Purple, Red, Yellow

5   All pale shades, Blue, Gray, Silver

6   Blue, Crimson, Green, Pink, Red, Rose, Wine

7   Blue, Gray, Green, White, Yellow

8   Black, Blue, Brown, Gray, Purple, White, Yellow

9   Blue, Coral, Mauve, Pink, Red, Rose, Scarlet, Wine

You will notice that blue appears advantageous to every number except Ones. Certainly blue deserves popularity --- being the color of the sky and, therefore, of the planet Jupiter. It is also the color of eternity, faith, purity, and modesty in Christian symbolism. The Virgin Mary's robe is usually blue, perhaps because of her role as the Queen of Heaven.

Wearing one of your compatible colors may add to the powers of your numbers while participating in games of chance.

COMPATIBLE NUMBERS

From time to time it is not possible or practical to use your own Personal Number and, therefore, it is wise to learn which numbers are compatible with it.

To find out if any number is compatible with your Personal Number, add all the digits together until you arrive at a 1-digit figure. Note that 0's are omitted in the calculations.

Should the test number be 10744, add 1 + 7 + 4 + 4. This total is 16. Add 1 + 6 which equals the primary number 7. Hence, the original 10744 could be fortunate for one whose Personal Number is 7.

If the number is 2946932, add 2 + 9 + 4 + 6 + 9 + 3 + 2 which totals 35. Add 3 plus 5 which results in the primary number 8, and could be advantageous for one whose Personal Number is 8.

Take the number 3711485069284. All digits add to a total of 58. 5 plus 8 equals 13. 1 plus 3 totals 4. Therefore, the conclusion is that the original 3711485069284 would possibly prove to be lucky for those whose Personal Number is 4.

The simplist illustration on compatible numbers may be for those who wager on horse races. While it is assumed that the horse is the most important consideration, the post position can also have a bearing on the results. Those who believe that a compatible number can bring extra strength to their luck in picking a winner may want to use the information in their selection.

COMPATIBLE STONES

Many authorities suggest that various gems have particular powers -- especially as lucky charms. Certain stones allegedly have special significance in relation to specific numbers.

If Your Personal Number Is:	Beneficial Stones
1	Amber, Diamond, Ruby, Topaz
2	Jade, Moonstone, Onyx, Pearl
3	Amethyst, Carbuncle, Emerald, Turquoise
4	Diamond, Ruby, Sapphire, Topaz
5	Diamond, Emerald, Hyacinth, Turquoise
6	Emerald, Opal, Turquoise
7	Cat's Eye, Jade, Moonstone, Moss Agate, Onyx, Pearl
8	Black Diamond, Black Pearl, Lapis Lazuli, Onyx
9	Amethyst, Bloodstone, Garnet, Ruby, Topaz

Carrying or wearing one of your lucky stones can prove beneficial while betting or taking part in any games of chance.

LOVE ATTRIBUTES

Some believe that one's number can provide clues as to sexuality or sexual compatibility. For those who wish to take notice of such information, given below are a few characteristics associated with each number.

One: Dependable, Controlling, Adventurous, Understanding

Two: Sensitive, Emotional, Thoughtful, Shy, Changeable

Three: Romantic, Flirty, Peace loving, Lively, Versatile

Four: Loyal, Dependable, Jealous, Kind, Affectionate

Five: Pleasure loving, Moody, Adventurous, Sensual, Restless

Six: Devoted, Home lover, Compassionate, Idealistic, Possessive, Stubborn

Seven: Shy, Thoughtful, Spiritual, Reserved, Perfectionist

Eight: Conscientious, Discreet, Dependable, Diplomatic

Nine: Moody, Considerate, Insecure, Romantic, Energetic

L

INNER SELF ATTRIBUTES

Everyone has wants, needs, ambitions, and desires which are many times never acknowledged or expressed. Perhaps this section will cause readers to bring forth these suppressed urges -- some good and some bad. They can then be accepted as part of one's being or make a conscious decision to eliminate them if they are destructive.

One: Prefers to work alone and be in complete charge. Is capable of great accomplishments. Can be critical and impatient of trivial blocks. Demands high achievement from friends and family. Seeks reinforcement and praise from others.

Two: Can be trusted to keep all secrets. Is emotional, falls in love easily and cries frequently. Loves music, art, and literature. Is easy going, relaxed, and not very ambitious.

Three: Takes life a day at a time without regret of the past or fear of the future. Loves children, pets, and animals. Never worries or mopes over mistakes of little consequence. Dreams of the stars but keeps feet on the ground.

Four: Seeks and needs respectability and solid values. Takes directions well, but does not want responsibility for important matters. Has great pride in family and friends.

Five: Adapts well to any unexpected condition. Enjoys new people, places, and things. Cannot submit to dull routines or small details. Has very little sense of responsibility.

Six: Is sensitive, kind, and understanding. Does not like to work alone. Wants love, domesticity, and security. Tries to right all wrongs, and improve other's lives.

Seven: Is secretive, reclusive, and very shy. Hates noise, confusion, and acrimony. Likes to be alone, but is not lonely. Loves old fashioned values, and conservative political views.

Eight: Is efficient, self-sufficient, and has excellent judgment. Is fond of money and nice things. Wants success in all material matters. Is generous to others and uses their abilities for goodness.

Nine: Gives to others often and generously. Has wisdom, and is attractive and loved by all. Is a dreamer with a passion for improving all things. Has the potential for benefitting mankind.

M

TALENTS
IN THE WORK PLACE

ONE's have a knack for buying and selling. They are inclined to be creative, and perform their duties best if left to carry out their own ideas. Their mental qualities enable them to become writers, executives, or lawyers.

TWO's usually tend to prefer occupations where they can work along with others rather than alone. They follow rather than lead, and are most comfortable in situations where details are important.

THREE's can be effective sales people because of their imaginative methods of presentation. They tend to be writers, musicians, or actors.

FOUR's prefer systematic, rather than creative, work. Their material gain is important to them, and they want organization, order, and accuracy.

FIVE's make the best salesmen for they are 'all things to all people.' They hate solitude and want freedom of speech and actions.

SIXES want positions of responsibility and trust. They seem to be very successful when their job is such that the work improves conditions, either materially or by education.

SEVEN's are the perfectionists who are at ease in a corporate office or any line of executive work. They are thinkers with ideas and prudent judgment.

EIGHT's are almost always drawn toward 'big business' and win because there is seldom any thought of limitations.

NINE's give freely of themselves to others, and work best in situations where kindliness, decency, consideration, and human understanding are essential.

Suggested Occupations

ONE   Inventor, Sales, Explorer, Editor, Attorney, Owner of any business

TWO   Teacher, Artist, Diplomat, Psychologist, Statistician, Secretary, Psychic

THREE   Poet, Writer, Entertainer, Clergyman, Jeweler, Singer, Actor, Musician

FOUR   Author, Professor, Scientist, Physician, Chemist, Electrician, Musician, Builder

FIVE   Civic Leader, Detective, Editor, Salesman, Writer, Courier, Lawyer

SIX   Musician, Doctor or Nurse, Teacher, Welfare Worker, Actor, Writer

SEVEN   Banker, Broker, Priest, Occultist, Watchmaker, Judge, Inventor, Scientist

EIGHT   Manufacturer, Corporation Executive Officer, Bondsman, Promoter

NINE   Teacher, Criminal Lawyer, Surgeon, Philanthropist, Actor, Artist, Composer, Statesman

YOUR NUMBER AND YOUR JOB

It seems that particular fields of endeavor may be more suitable for certain people than for others. Some believe that your personal number might well be considered when searching for work. The following are merely suggestions which one may wish to investigate and consider for a career.

If Your Personal Number Is	Check out these opportunities when searching for work.
One:	A vocation which offers opportunities to put into use these qualities -- leadership, determination, creativity, initiative, and the ability to work alone without constant supervision.
Two:	A workplace which will allow you to use your diplomacy, cooperation, dedication to details, and expansion of your field of expertise.
Three:	Your artistic talents, a sense of humor, and ability to sort the important from the insignificant can add to your value.
Four:	Dependability, loyalty, self-discipline, and thoroughness will provide opportunities to progress rapidly.
Five:	Personal charm, salesmanship, contact with the public, and varied situation may lead to a quick offer of a more lucrative position.
Six:	Use your courage and strength to better conditions in the work place. Make the necessary adjustments without complaint. Rewards will come later.
Seven:	Take charge when appropriate, and carry out orders as required. It will gain you friends and allies.
Eight:	Expand your horizons and use the provided opportunities to enhance your management potential.
Nine:	A position which includes contact with people will not only be of monetary value to you, but will nourish your inner needs to enrich and comfort others.

LUCKY AND UNLUCKY DATES

According to the Grand Grimoire, there are certain days of the year which are simply lucky or unlucky, and for those who wish to consider this ancient knowledge and be guided by it, these are listed below.

Month	Lucky Dates	Unlucky Dates
JANUARY	3, 10, 27, 31	12, 23
FEBRUARY	7, 8, 18	2, 10, 17, 22
MARCH	3, 9, 12, 14, 16	13, 19, 23, 28
APRIL	5, 17	18, 20, 29, 30
MAY	1, 2, 4, 6, 9	10, 17, 20
JUNE	3, 5, 7, 9, 13, 23	4, 20
JULY	3, 6, 10, 23, 30	5, 13, 27
AUGUST	5, 7, 10, 14	2, 13, 27, 31
SEPTEMBER	6, 10, 18, 30	13, 16, 19
OCTOBER	13, 16, 25, 31	3, 9, 27
NOVEMBER	1, 13, 23, 30	6, 25
DECEMBER	10, 20, 29	15, 26

DREAMS AND NUMBERS

This section cannot be considered anything more than a quick cursory survey of some common dreams and the numbers associated with these particular subjects.

---A---					
ABANDONMENT	247	BALL	381	BURIAL	598
ABDOMEN	465	BALLOON	134	BUS	339
ABILITY	231	BANANA	257	BUTCHER	055
ABORTION	107	BANK	072	BUTTER	952
ABSENCE	310	BANQUET	006	BUTTON	210
ABSTINENCE	285	BAR	787	BUZZARD	196
ABUNDANCE	353	BARBER	804	---C---	
ABUSE	434	BASEMENT	122	CABBAGE	441
ABYSS	042	BAT	211	CACTUS	268
ACCEPTANCE	790	BATH	530	CAGE	074
ACCIDENT	922	BATTLE	089	CAKE	611
ACCORDION	509	BEACH	289	CAMERA	390
ACE	116	BEADS	261	CAMPFIRE	212
ACORN	668	BEANS	689	CANCER	614
ADOPTION	996	BEARD	835	CANDLE	483
ADORNMENT	508	BED	484	CANDY	215
ADULTERY	774	BEEF	017	CANOE	070
ADVICE	918	BEER	204	CANYON	653
AGE	136	BEES	363	CAR	885
AIRPLANE	010	BELLS	474	CARDS	287
ALCOHOL	671	BEST MAN	190	CARNIVAL	201
ALIBI	829	BIBLE	721	CAROUSEL	949
ALIMONY	990	BILL	321	CARPENTER	110
ALMANAC	625	BINOCULARS	909	CARTON	538
AMBITION	798	BIRDS	508	CASTLE	869
AMBULANCE	210	BIRTHDAY	166	CAT	543
ANESTHESIA	662	BITE	819	CATERPILLAR	161
ANCESTORS	734	BLACKBIRD	077	CAVE	053
ANCHOR	163	BLAZE	392	CELEBRATION	884
ANGEL	349	BLOOD	932	CEMETERY	602
ANGER	006	BOAT	507	CEREAL	339
ANNIVERSARY	444	BONDS	318	CHAINS	757
APOLOGY	530	BONES	585	CHAIR	680
APPLAUSE	372	BOOK	442	CHAMPAGNE	184
ARCADE	905	BOOT	597	CHANT	673
ARENA	189	BOSS	904	CHARCOAL	306
ARREST	298	BOTTLES	226	CHECK	090
ASHES	868	BOUQUET	390	CHEESE	219
ASSISTANCE	539	BRACELET	167	CHESTNUT	410
ATTIC	811	BREAD	923	CHILDREN	368
AUDITORIUM	346	BRIDE	600	CHOCOLATE	075
AUTOMOBILE	225	BRIDEGROOM	187	CHORUS	325
AXE	713	BRIEFCASE	702	CHRISTMAS	648
---B---		BRIMSTONE	406	CHURCH	707
BABY	714	BROOM	542	CIRCLE	099
BACHELOR	392	BRUISE	063	CLARINET	214
BACON	749	BRUSH	917	CLOCK	939
BAGGAGE	918	BUCKET	818	CLOTHES	440
BAIL	179	BUCKLE	230	CLOUD	925
BAKERY	963	BULL	775	COAL	316
BALDNESS	172	BURDEN	929	COAT	678
		BURGLAR	376	COBWEB	905

COCONUT	271	**---E---**		GERMS	518
COFFEE	690	EAGLE	998	GIFT	129
COFFIN	218	EARRINGS	891	GINGER	709
COLD	413	EARTHQUAKE	449	GIRL	881
COMMITTEE	173	EATING	104	GLASS	869
CONCERT	592	EGG	193	GLOVE	764
CONSPIRACY	060	ELEPHANT	386	GOAT	329
CONTEST	797	ELEVATOR	927	GOD	750
COPPER	668	ELM	797	GOLD	388
CORAL	132	EMERALD	909	GOOSE	413
CORD	786	ENEMY	582	GORILLA	083
CORN	158	ENVELOPE	913	GOURD	304
CORPSE	992	EPITAPH	800	GRAIN	456
COSTUME	525	ERASER	208	GRANDPARENT	574
COTTON	929	EVIL SPIRITS	065	GRASS	806
COUGH	872	EYES	437	GREASE	349
COUPON	881	**---F---**		GROUND HOG	308
COWARD	609	FACE	293	GUEST	934
COYOTE	335	FAIRY	456	GUN	829
CRADLE	068	FALCON	417	GYPSY	792
CREEK	219	FAMILY	102	**---H---**	
CRICKET	984	FAN	334	HAIR	484
CROSS	002	FARM	646	HALF MOON	033
CRUCIFIX	748	FATHER	445	HALO	457
CRYSTAL	443	FAWN	311	HAM	406
CURTAIN	178	FEAST	670	HAMMER	298
CYCLONE	493	FENCE	259	HAND	333
---D---		FERN	752	HANGER	578
DAGGER	681	FEET	734	HARBOR	180
DAISY	818	FESTIVAL	132	HARNESS	426
DANCERS	707	FEVER	386	HASH	803
DANGER	336	FIELD	616	HAT	379
DAUGHTER	098	FINGER	691	HATCHET	994
DEBTS	315	FIRE	180	HAWK	305
DEED	547	FISH	240	HAY	626
DENTIST	894	FLAG	919	HEAD	400
DETOUR	392	FLOOD	772	HEADLINE	105
DEVIL	802	FLOUR	401	HEADSTONE	638
DIAMONDS	691	FLY	260	HEARSE	919
DICE	306	FOOD	082	HEART	953
DINNER	899	FOOT	588	HEAT	579
DIRT	852	FORK	917	HEAVEN	582
DISORDER	605	FORTUNE TELLER	740	HEDGE	825
DIVORCE	115	FOUNTAIN PEN	120	HEEL	357
DOG	701	FRIEND	894	HELL	415
DONKEY	689	FROG	662	HELP	789
DOORBELL	914	FUNERAL	298	HEN	706
DOVE	125	FUR	038	HERO	251
DRAGON	376	FUTURE	689	HICCOUGH	952
DRESS	097	**---G---**		HILL	410
DRIVING	358	GALE	847	HIVE	921
DROWNING	221	GAME	209	HOAX	496
DRUM	822	GANG	509	HOBO	148
DUCK	492	GARDEN	492	HOE	093
DUST	334	GARNET	723	HOG	822
DWARF	513	GARTER	491	HOLE	449
DYNAMITE	495	GATE	395	HOLIDAY	856

HOLLY	127	LADDER	701	MINE	902
HOME	606	LAKE	541	MINISTER	348
HONEYMOON	902	LAMP	296	MIRACLE	555
HOOK	539	LANDLORD	159	MIRROR	339
HORN	212	LAP	314	MISTLETOE	809
HORSE	044	LAUGHTER	226	MOB	203
HORSESHOE	777	LAUNDRY	408	MOLASSES	560
HOSPITAL	339	LAVENDER	297	MONEY	777
HOTEL	942	LAW	179	MOON	396
HOUSE	908	LAWYER	097	MOONSTONE	740
HUNGER	409	LEAF	818	MOP	133
HUNTING	427	LEASE	232	MORGUE	436
HUSBAND	535	LEG	515	MORTGAGE	507
---I---		LEMON	624	MOTHER	820
ICE	284	LETTER	091	MOUNTAIN	966
IDOL	902	LIE	962	MOUSE	564
INCENSE	817	LIGHTNING	330	MUD	430
INDIAN	646	LINEN	184	MULE	106
INFIDELITY	380	LION	727	MUMMY	089
INHERITANCE	618	LIVER	923	MURDER	571
INK	370	LOAN	097	MUSEUM	696
INSECT	562	LOCK	110	MUSTACHE	205
INSURANCE	433	LOCKET	528	---N---	
INVALID	790	LORD'S PRAYER	374	NAIL	160
INVITATION	885	LOTTERY	580	NAPKIN	355
ISLAND	159	LOVE	216	NECKLACE	278
ITCH	296	LUCK	707	NEIGHBOR	540
IVORY	974	LYNCHING	491	NEST	371
IVY	307	---M---		NEWSPAPER	596
---J---		MACHINERY	051	NICKEL	126
JACKET	685	MAD DOG	923	NOSE	301
JADE	212	MAGAZINE	976	NUMBERS	238
JAIL	604	MAGIC	184	NURSE	300
JAR	641	MAGNET	399	NUT	406
JAW	299	MAIL	482	---O---	
JEALOUSY	030	MAN	126	OATH	801
JESUS	546	MANUSCRIPT	453	OBITUARY	666
JEWELRY	838	MAP	100	OCEAN	607
JOB	617	MARATHON	890	ODOR	572
JOKE	039	MARBLES	574	OFFICER	472
JOURNEY	045	MARKET	318	OINTMENT	717
JUDAS	474	MARRIAGE	740	OLIVES	837
JUDGE	202	MASK	255	ONION	208
JUGGLER	991	MASSAGE	929	ONYX	225
JUNK	135	MATCH	527	OPAL	066
JUSTICE	470	MATE	046	OPERATION	745
---K---		MATTRESS	374	ORANGE	950
KALEIDOSCOPE	533	MAYOR	214	ORCHESTRA	944
KEY	602	MEADOW	202	ORGAN	322
KIDNAPPING	100	MEAT	724	ORNAMENT	409
KING	802	MEDAL	207	OUTLAW	509
KISS	707	MEDICINE	620	OVEN	719
KITE	460	MELON	137	OWL	269
KITTEN	678	MERCURY	289	OYSTER	751
KNEE	561	MERRY-GO-		---P---	
KNIFE	327	ROUND	433	PACKAGE	235
KNOCK	386	MESSENGER	567	PADLOCK	479
KNOT	952	METER	651	PAIL	501
---L---		MICROSCOPE	207		
LACE	308	MILK	492		

PAIN	874	PRESENT	193	ROBIN	182
PAINT	210	PRIEST	689	ROCKER	219
PALLBEARER	864	PRINCE	565	ROLLING PIN	411
PAN	885	PRINCESS	998	ROOF	337
PANTHER	309	POISON	102	ROOSTER	019
PAPER	421	PRIZE	538	ROPE	544
PARACHUTE	125	PROPOSAL	660	ROSE	868
PARADE	220	PUBLISHER	312	ROULETTE	938
PARCEL	808	PULPIT	825	RUBBER	109
PARK	298	PUMP	747	RUBBISH	257
PARSON	363	PUMPKIN	705	RUBY	795
PARTNER	276	PUPPY	599	RUG	367
PARTY	978	PYRAMID	376	RUMMAGE SALE	607
PASTRY	122	---Q---		RUPTURE	397
PATH	322	QUAIL	383	RYE	321
PATTERN	457	QUARTZ	129	---S---	
PAWNBROKER	908	QUEEN	044	SABBATH	914
PEACOCK	755	QUICKSAND	635	SABLE	545
PEAR	704	QUILT	696	SACHET	508
PEARL	126	QUIZ	578	SADDLE	103
PEN	310	QUOTATION	263	SAILOR	742
PENNY	723	---R---		SALARY	594
PEPPER	103	RABBI	919	SALE	732
PERFUME	526	RABBIT	774	SALOON	457
PHEASANT	503	RACE	424	SALT	501
PHONOGRAPH	308	RADIO	096	SAND	624
PHOTOGRAPH	668	RAFFLE	167	SANDWICH	703
PIANO	795	RAID	574	SANITARIUM	630
PICNIC	243	RAIN	694	SAPPHIRE	129
PIG	939	RAINBOW	648	SAW	928
PILL	508	RAKE	329	SCAFFOLD	374
PILLOW	073	RANCH	049	SCALES	420
PIN	213	RANSOM	896	SCAR	829
PINE	644	RAPE	326	SCARF	705
PINEAPPLE	237	RAT	576	SCHOOL	066
PIPE	846	RATTLE	727	SCISSORS	204
PISTOL	714	RATTLESNAKE	389	SCORE	687
PITCHER	975	RAZOR	035	SCRAPBOOK	530
PLAGUE	218	REAL ESTATE	130	SEAHORSE	329
PLATE	173	RECIPE	785	SEAL	801
PLAY	810	RECORD	386	SEANCE	398
PLUMBING	341	REFRIGERATOR	522	SECRET	926
POCKETBOOK	029	REINDEER	957	SECRETARY	560
POEM	257	RELIGION	216	SEWING	102
POET	259	RENT	614	SEX	840
POISON	400	RESTAURANT	908	SHAMROCK	790
POLICE	794	RETIREMENT	322	SHAWL	225
POLICY	908	REVENGE	484	SHEEP	372
POND	315	REVOLVER	505	SHELL	836
POOL	408	REWARD	167	SHERIFF	284
PORCH	281	RIBBON	802	SHIP	369
PORK	981	RICE	215	SHOE	209
PORTER	438	RIFLE	907	SHOVEL	108
PORTRAIT	221	RING	051	SIGNATURE	452
POSTMAN	162	RIOT	843	SILO	135
POTATO	817	RIVAL	343	SIN	903
POWDER	947	RIVER	145	SISTER	340
PRAYER	098	ROAST	497	SKELETON	496
PREGNANCY	381	ROBBERY	246	SKULL	971

SKUNK	236	TEACHER	396	VIOLIN	680
SLIP	072	TELEGRAM	696	VISITOR	762
SMOKE	913	TELEPHONE	617	VOLCANO	702
SNAIL	882	TELEVISION	302	VOW	435
SNAKE	124	TENT	401	VOYAGE	706
SNOW	286	THANKSGIVING	840	**---W---**	
SOAP	582	THEATER	756	WAGON	622
SOFA	321	THIEF	108	WAITER	806
SON	618	THIMBLE	514	WALLET	513
SOUP	308	THORN	397	WALLPAPER	137
SPAGHETTI	742	THREAD	187	WAND	909
SPARROW	425	THUMB	325	WAR	629
SPHINX	489	THUNDER	226	WAREHOUSE	951
SPIDER	898	TIDE	808	WASHING	736
SPLINTER	184	TIGER	823	WATCH	355
SPONGE	686	TIRE	602	WATER	518
SPOON	311	TOAD	397	WATERFALL	944
SPUR	782	TOBACCO	849	WATERMELON	460
SQUIRREL	967	TOILET	164	WAX	453
STADIUM	271	TONGUE	327	WEB	415
STAGE	158	TOOL	362	WEDDING	802
STAIN	947	TOOTH	268	WHALE	920
STAIRS	326	TORCH	691	WHEEL	457
STAMP	493	TOWEL	423	WHIP	134
STAR	763	TRAIN	658	WHISKERS	459
STATUE	542	TRAMP	120	WHISTLE	222
STEEL	281	TRAVEL	327	WIDOW	442
STEEPLE	449	TREADMILL	556	WIG	718
STEW	257	TREE	804	WIND	506
STOCKING	886	TRIAL	117	WINDOW	449
STORE	922	TROPHY	215	WINE	201
STORM	529	TRUCK	402	WISHBONE	445
STOVE	774	TRUNK	405	WITCH	666
STUTTER	604	TULIP	603	WOLF	924
SUITCASE	462	TWEEZERS	289	WREATH	613
SUNDIAL	381	TWINE	803	WRECK	583
SUNRISE	048	**---U---**		WRITER	529
SUNSET	036	ULCER	508	**---X---**	
SUSPENDERS	546	UMBRELLA	049	X-RAYS	069
SWAMP	491	UMPIRE	404	XYLOPHONE	421
SWEATER	210	UNDERTAKER	999	**---Y---**	
SWIMMING	382	UNIFORM	090	YACHT	603
SWORD	797	URN	107	YARDSTICK	180
SYNAGOGUE	574	USHER	794	YARN	647
---T---		**---V---**		YAWN	849
TABLE	909	VALENTINE	229	YELL	216
TACK	196	VAMPIRE	190	YELLOW	449
TAILOR	411	VASE	913	YOKE	205
TAMBOURINE	472	VAULT	779	YOUTH	944
TANTRUM	310	VEIL	423	**---Z---**	
TARANTULA	710	VEIN	155	ZEBRA	221
TATTOO	204	VEST	852	ZEPHYR	245
TAX	378	VINE	402	ZERO	040
TEA	454	VIOLET	923	ZODIAC	697

MEANING OF A FEW
SIGNIFICANT DREAMS

ACCIDENT ...... Warning of danger
ADULTERY .... Guilt feelings
ALTAR .... Sacrifice
ANCHOR .... Strong attachments
AXE .... Argument with friends
BABY .... Contentment
BALL .... Wide horizons
BARBER .... Reckless actions
BEACH .... Serenity, Balance
BED .... Love and comfort
BIRDS .... High ideals
BRACELET .... Reunion
CAGE .... Restrictions
CANDLE .... Spiritual light
CASTLE .... Prosperity
CAT .... Good times ahead
CLIFF .... Obstacle ahead
CROSS .... Protection
DAM .... Emotional block
DEATH .... Changing times
DOVE .... Peace of mind
EARTHQUAKE ..... Change, Chaos
ENVELOPE ...... Beware of danger
EYES .... Psychic sight
FAMINE .... Hard times coming
FIELDS .... Simplify your life
FLOOD .... Emotional turmoil
FRUIT .... Rewards on the way
GATE .... Make new paths
GRAIN .... Reward for work
GUEST .... Unexpected callers
HAIR .... Sexual power
HAND .... Fate
HANDCUFFS .... Obstacles
HARVEST .... Success
HEATHER .... Good fortune
HORSE .... Increased energy
HUNGER .... Dissatisfaction
ILLNESS ..... Take care of yourself
IRON .. Strenth & endurance needed
JESUS .. Divine blessings, Protection
JOURNEY .... Travel and change
KEY .... Clue to a problem
KNIFE .... Beware of enemies
KNOT .... Keep it simple
LAKE .... Smooth sailing
LANTERN .... A warning sign
LETTER .... Unexpected news
LIFT .... Better times coming
LOCK .... Obstacle in your path

LOST .... Insecurity, Uncertainty
MIRROR .. Look inward for answers
MONEY .. Improved financial matters
MOVE .... Change is anticipated
MUSEUM ..... Old friends may arrive
NAIL .... Be persistent in your goals
NEEDLE .. Watch your sharp tongue
NEST ...... Protection from enemies
NIGHTINGALE .. A new lover in sight
OCEAN .... Rocky times ahead
ORCHIDS .... Passionate love
OWL .. Escape from a serious threat
PARENTS ... Harmony in your home
PENCIL .... Health and wealth
PLUM .... Joyous occasion soon
PRAYER .... Help is coming
PYRAMID .... Success at the top
QUARRY ... A promotion is possible
QUICKSAND .... Loss is coming
QUILT ... Comfortable circumstances
RAIN .... Disappointment
RAT .... Victory over foe
RAZOR .... Bad luck to come
REVENGE .... Loss of prestige
RIBBON .... Easy times
RIVAL .... Loss of contest
SATAN .... Dangerous risks
SCISSORS .... Separations
SHAVING .... Beware of plots
SHELLS .... Save for the future
SHROUD ..... Sickness and distress
SKELETON .... Misunderstanding
SNAKE .... Beware of enemy
SPIDER .... Good fortune
TEETH .... Be careful
TENT .... Changes coming
THUNDER .... Business loss
TORNADO .... Disappointment
TUNNEL .... Unpleasant trip
UMBRELLA ...... Missunderstanding
UNIFORM .... Ill health
VALLEY .... Business improves
VEIL .... Separation
VINE .... Good health
VOLCANO .... Confusion
WAGON .... Secret revealed
WALLET .... Money coming
WARTS .... Beware of enemy
WATER .... Pleasure and prosperity
WEATHER .... Change coming

R

CARDS AND THEIR NUMBERS

To find your lucky numbers with cards is quite simple and by using the method given below you will be able to quickly select those which fit in with your needs.

Use this method only on the day on which you intend to use it, and reserve the deck for this special purpose only.

Shuffle the cards thoroughly. Then sort the deck into three piles, face down on the table.

Select one pile, and divide it into three piles -- face down. Choose one of the three piles and spread the cards -- still face down -- to form a circle. Quickly select one of the cards from the circle and turn it face up.

From the following lists, find the chosen card with its specific lucky number.

CLUBS		DIAMONDS	
TWO	30	TWO	91
THREE	72	THREE	84
FOUR	8	FOUR	18
FIVE	65	FIVE	6
SIX	15	SIX	73
SEVEN	48	SEVEN	34
EIGHT	10	EIGHT	71
NINE	27	NINE	80
TEN	94	TEN	14
JOKER	69	JOKER	49
JACK	36	JACK	23
QUEEN	81	QUEEN	65
KING	34	KING	57
ACE	23	ACE	2

HEARTS		SPADES	
TWO	89	TWO	35
THREE	49	THREE	57
FOUR	28	FOUR	16
FIVE	9	FIVE	93
SIX	20	SIX	81
SEVEN	35	SEVEN	97
EIGHT	63	EIGHT	19
INE	91	NINE	64
TEN	45	TEN	28
JOKER	96	JOKER	82
JACK	14	JACK	33
QUEEN	17	QUEEN	42
KING	3	KING	78
ACE	56	ACE	45

GOOD HEALTH
AND HERBAL REMEDIES

Just as there are various diseases that are associated with persons born under the numbers that make their birth date, so there are particular herbs, plants, vegetables, and fruits which correspond to similar conditions. They often can alleviate the illness.

Number 1 persons may suffer from heart trouble, high blood pressure, or eye problems.
> *HERBS & FRUITS: Camomile, Bay Leaves, Nutmeg, Dates, Thyme, Myrrh, Vervain, Ginger, Barley, Honey*

Number 2 persons have a tendency to suffer with ailments of the stomach and digestive organs.
> *HERBS & FRUITS: Lettuce, Cabbage, Melon, Moonwort, Plantain, Endive, Linseed, Turnips*

Number 3 persons often overstrain the nervous system by overwork, and they are inclined to have skin troubles, neuritis, and sciatica.
> *HERBS & FRUITS: Beets, Asparagus, Endive, Sage, Cherries, Apples, Olives, St. John's Wort, Almonds, Figs, Wheat*

Number 4 persons are likely to suffer from mysterious ailments, often difficult to diagnosis. They should avoid drugs if possible.
> *HERBS & FRUITS: Spinach, Sage, Wintergreen, Solomon's Seal*

Number 5 persons often overstrain their nervous system, attempt too much mentally, and bring on nervous prostration and insomnia.
> *HERBS & FRUITS: Carrots, Oatmeal, Bread, Parsley, Caraway Seeds, Thyme, Nuts of all kinds.*

Number 6 persons may suffer with nose, throat, and lung diseases.
> *HERBS & FRUITS: Beans, Mint, Spinach, Almonds, Melons, Thyme, Violets, Vervain, and Rose Leaves*

Number 7 people are easily affected by worry and annoyance, and tend to imagine things are worse than they really are, bringing on melancholy and despondency.

> *HERBS & FRUITS: Angelica, Shepherd's Purse, Celery, Marshmallow, Sage, Wild Carrot, Elder Flowers*

Number 8 persons are prone to trouble with the liver, bile, and intestines, as well as suffering with headaches and rheumatism.

> *HERBS & FRUITS: Spinach, Gravel Root, Elder Flowers, Sage, Gravel Root, Wintergreen*

Number 9 persons are inclined to fevers of all kinds, measles, chicken-pox, and must guard against ill-health during April, May, October, and November.

> *HERBS & FRUITS: Garlic, Wormwood, Ginger, Hops, Betony, Pepper, Hops, and juice of Nettles.*

The months to be most guarded against for ill-health are April, May, October, and November. The years in which changes in health are most likely are the ninth, eighteenth, twenty-seventh, thirty-sixth, forty-fifth, fifty-fourth, sixty-third, and seventy-second.

CHINESE HOROSCOPE
or The Wheel of Life

According to ancient history, Buddha once asked all the world's animals to come to visit him. At the appointed time, only twelve responded so, in their honor, he created the Chinese Horoscope or Wheel of Life.

There are twelve signs which change yearly rather than monthly, and a particular animal represents each period.

The following chart covers the time period from 1900 through 2079. Beginning the next year, 2080, the cycle would repeat from 2080 during the next one hundred eighty years.

1900,	1912,	1924,	1936,	1948,	1960,	1972,	1984,	RAT
1996,	2008,	2020,	2032,	2044,	2056,	2068,	etc.	
1901,	1913,	1925,	1937,	1949,	1961,	1973,	1985,	BULL
1997,	2009,	2021,	2033,	2045,	2057,	2069,	etc.	
1902,	1914,	1926,	1938,	1950,	1962,	1974,	1986,	TIGER
1998,	2010,	2022,	2034,	2046,	2058,	2070,	etc.	
1903,	1915,	1927,	1939,	1951,	1963,	1975,	1987,	HARE
1999,	2011,	2023,	2035,	2047,	2059,	2071,	etc.	
1904,	1916,	1928,	1940,	1952,	1964,	1976,	1988,	DRAGON
2000,	2012,	2024,	2036,	2048,	2060,	2072,	etc.	
1905,	1917,	1929,	1941,	1953,	1965,	1977,	1989,	SNAKE
2001,	2013,	2025,	2037,	2049,	2061,	2073,	etc.	
1906,	1918,	1930,	1942,	1954,	1966,	1978,	1990,	HORSE
2002,	2014,	2026,	2038,	2050,	2062,	2074,	etc.	
1907,	1919,	1931,	1943,	1955,	1967,	1979,	1991,	RAM
2003,	2015,	2027,	2039,	2051,	2063,	2075,	etc.	
1908,	1920,	1932,	1944,	1956,	1968,	1980,	1992,	MONKEY
2004,	2016,	2028,	2040,	2052,	2064,	2076,	etc.	
1909,	1921,	1933,	1945,	1957,	1969,	1981,	1993,	ROOSTER
2005,	2017,	2029,	2041,	2053,	2065,	2077,	etc.	
1910,	1922,	1934,	1946,	1958,	1970,	1982,	1994,	DOG
2006,	2018,	2030,	2042,	2054,	2066,	2078,	etc.	
1911,	1923,	1935,	1947,	1959,	1971,	1983,	1995,	BOAR
2007,	2019,	2031,	2043,	2055,	2067,	2079,	etc.	

The inherent characteristics usually found in those born under each of the various signs are given for those who wish to consider them.

1	BOAR	Noble, chivalrous, faithful friend
2	BULL	Patient, strong, inspiring to others
3	DOG	Generous, outgoing, courageous
4	DRAGON	Essentric, passionate, healthy
5	HARE	Talented, articulate, shy
6	HORSE	Loves animals, popular with opposite sex
7	MONKEY	Intelligent, influential, like to travel
8	RAM	Artistic, creative, shy
9	RAT	Ambitious, honest, a spendthrift
10	ROOSTER	Seeker of truth, hard worker, helpful to others
11	SNAKE	Wise, intense, physically attractive
12	TIGER	Aggressive, courageous, melancholy

SIGNIFICANCE
OF NUMBERS

Each number has particular qualities and often these explanations give one insight into their problems. They reveal why one is more compatible with certain persons than with others, or they guide one toward selecting a career or understanding of a shortcoming.

ONE   This is the number of creation, energy, boldness, beginnings, strength. Ones are leaders, thinkers, pioneers. They are filled with vigor and desire for action, but are more suited to meeting immediate situations than to planning for the future. Ones are the first to be called on to deliver, and the first to be blamed when they can't, even though someone else may be the cause of the failure. These people usually are successful in financial dealings, but they spend the money they make freely. Many Ones are eccentric, egotistical, self-centered, and should avoid making hasty decisions under the excitement of the moment.

TWO   The number of beauty, culture, perception, consciousness. Twos make warm, loyal friends and are kind, peace loving, tactful, and good judges of human nature. They are overgenerous and often give to others, thereby neglecting their own needs. They have a need for balance which leads them to recognize and consider both sides of a situation -- sometimes to such a degree that they find it hard to make a definite decision. Twos should avoid worry over small matters, seldom if ever indulge in arguments, and simply make the most of their agreeable, friendly qualities.

THREE The number of refinement, enlightenment, thoroughness. Threes are affectionate, cautious, sympathetic, fun loving, cheerful, and idealistic. They have abilities of many kinds, are usually good at public speaking, acting, singing, writing, dancing, or painting. Threes are energetic, with little patience for trivial problems.

FOUR   The number of stability, security, reliability, and endurance. Fours are sometimes hard to understand and usually handle problems and their affairs in a way which is different from others. They feel that rules are made to be broken, and this can cause others to regard them as peculiar or strange. You have a few good, loyal friends and do not worry about those who are standoffish.

FIVE   The number of change, movement, and impulse. Fives are good judges of character and select a few close friends rather than many casual ones. They are perfectionists, and only the best of everything is good enough for them. As long as there is excitement and challenges, they are happy.

SIX   The number of magnetism, the arts, love, and sex. With a magnetic personality, lucky in money matters, and attractive to the opposite sex, life can be a bowl of cherries. Sixes, however, tend to be skeptics, miserly, and self-centered. As long as they are aware of these tendencies and keep them in perspective, their lives will be truly blessed.

SEVEN   The number of wisdom, mysticism, and success. Sevens are creative, intellectual, studious, and desirous of the finer things in life. They are naturally fond of the occult and the mysterious and, as a result, may become moody and depressed from time to time. These persons can direct their natural talents toward art, science, or philosophy, often attaining prominence in their chosen profession. While sevens are quite capable of solving intricate problems, they seldom truly understand themselves.

EIGHT   The number of evolution, justice, strength, genius, and business success. Eights have strong personalities, good business acumen, are very active, and excel in technical and scientific fields. They are willing to take risks to gain their objectives, and usually become well known in their chosen profession.

NINE   The number of efficiency, dominance, consciousness, and humanitarianism. Nines have universal love, are unusually psychic, often possessing telepathic minds. They are even tempered, have a fertile imagination, and often possess poetic or artistic talents. They are born aggressors, and have few, if any, fears.

NOTE

In this book there are directions on how to establish your own individual Birth Number and Name Number. But, should you need assistance, Miss Riva will do it for you --- FREE! Send your full name and date of birth on a letter size sheet of paper -- along with a STAMPED, SELF-ADDRESSED envelope for a prompt reply.

INDEX TO
PERSONAL NUMBERS
YOUR LUCKY NUMBERS . . . FOREVER!

Notice

This chart covers the years 1991 through 1999. After that, the cycle repeats itself. In 2000, use the information given for 1991. In the year 2001, use the 1992 pages, and onward with the cycle as shown. Hence -- here are *Your Lucky Numbers . . . Forever!*

JANUARY	2-DIGIT	3-DIGIT	4-DIGIT	5-DIGIT	6-DIGIT
1:	70	087	4214	04823	173046
2:	88	365	5927	73018	645470
3:	23	046	4528	48362	962236
4:	02	922	3982	46165	006832
5:	27	463	2984	55514	922107
6:	83	540	2038	16680	526267
7:	80	566	1642	54006	009943
8:	23	469	9478	92462	755878
9:	29	902	4089	67811	822981
10:	42	188	5049	53313	512475
11:	17	823	7678	23640	137962
12:	30	633	7508	83807	364395
13:	63	077	1027	62911	028806
14:	21	841	7872	06141	329254
15:	83	188	0475	48237	828042
16:	47	489	5852	65739	149826
17:	44	843	1253	91017	349946
18:	22	115	3154	53563	886331
19:	37	794	3939	84492	641035
20:	96	978	2025	91708	508717
21:	84	033	8794	78598	203209
22:	27	490	4333	34623	067070
23:	26	169	5381	39198	322364
24:	26	333	5388	33617	600308
25:	73	344	1630	49490	346225
26:	93	528	5638	22448	412058
27:	23	499	8179	84871	274678
28:	65	444	2929	29096	768411
29:	39	660	2207	35437	932132
30:	26	762	8926	50809	068329
31:	80	049	2282	01937	085195

FEBRUARY	2-DIGIT	3-DIGIT	4-DIGIT	5-DIGIT	6-DIGIT
1:	08	447	1931	07208	979812
2:	72	435	5626	54066	315471
3:	07	070	5758	58520	351227
4:	35	757	3092	68625	671780
5:	94	811	2659	14988	068913
6:	80	565	5726	83304	892670
7:	71	330	0136	40954	147956
8:	15	573	2113	14418	383204
9:	13	595	0777	01059	598372
10:	35	186	0055	85686	959159
11:	68	521	6586	82359	175600
12:	57	728	7772	61091	173673
13:	08	196	6498	48482	287242
14:	74	398	5601	30479	858754
15:	14	526	9660	25024	376360
16:	16	969	4033	21323	873814
17:	19	773	0827	48231	511807
18:	21	275	2251	73771	014362
19:	05	991	4704	76964	771535
20:	06	804	2489	84058	287885
21:	38	775	3449	78095	043856
22:	06	865	6466	58461	611596
23:	43	959	8907	96290	672466
24:	76	713	7634	56702	193783
25:	88	415	6950	13228	206935
26:	71	189	7608	56455	020630
27:	47	127	6034	96289	836784
28:	35	259	1586	54567	448500
29:	44	089	0488	36690	720101

MARCH	2-DIGIT	3-DIGIT	4-DIGIT	5-DIGIT	6-DIGIT
1:	66	910	8236	11658	248968
2:	39	742	5519	15988	907068
3:	37	951	3907	35248	307968
4:	44	120	5105	99802	461643
5:	29	238	1900	28723	033161
6:	26	286	2935	33677	487994
7:	87	718	3832	69754	516198
8:	88	114	6410	84994	070175
9:	76	254	4899	65736	113440
10:	23	706	9861	44969	366272
11:	37	268	8198	60466	932774
12:	90	245	6774	98425	147963
13:	72	494	0143	35374	425900
14:	62	583	8355	30291	129121
15:	33	779	5840	74017	769673
16:	65	158	2596	48108	821779
17:	10	465	0281	37131	669333
18:	31	945	7050	67432	337393
19:	95	298	3217	63854	317972
20:	28	685	8957	81608	981088
21:	70	966	9804	78410	621633
22:	57	319	9585	31545	631043
23:	52	848	9691	91336	947847
24:	66	630	1730	33306	910862
25:	32	346	0833	63978	139792
26:	13	891	4064	16240	412718
27:	31	422	4359	94092	897642
28:	97	876	6523	13852	447833
29:	79	245	7332	06513	159909
30:	49	031	2546	91395	269637
31:	88	201	2891	49300	590269

APRIL	2-DIGIT	3-DIGIT	4-DIGIT	5-DIGIT	6-DIGIT
1:	18	595	0381	55822	141063
2:	96	205	2483	49867	239592
3:	75	114	2238	20193	029395
4:	36	469	7075	78225	510546
5:	25	587	4133	80792	688123
6:	53	615	6034	72949	553218
7:	84	003	5350	38010	738316
8:	61	231	7452	80729	494264
9:	70	558	7433	08772	144855
10:	59	896	7138	48358	613476
11:	01	663	9566	43776	597782
12:	20	558	0852	13602	672398
13:	25	122	2928	49804	210050
14:	40	602	7589	53881	770281
15:	67	036	1347	12036	898873
16:	35	282	1303	03313	250820
17:	81	762	6166	00743	872539
18:	63	051	8920	64672	769054
19:	03	142	0055	83053	117234
20:	18	102	6787	84246	303656
21:	06	144	7157	76904	883848
22:	92	429	9233	63794	012444
23:	43	083	3732	15550	385739
24:	64	110	0801	77596	772833
25:	95	696	1975	80417	969136
26:	78	105	1643	31672	193139
27:	24	038	9102	65611	021833
28:	79	849	0802	12472	679926
29:	21	137	1159	21322	143599
30:	79	424	4779	56643	766524

MAY	2-DIGIT	3-DIGIT	4-DIGIT	5-DIGIT	6-DIGIT
1:	06	701	7514	64041	333651
2:	96	948	2665	80417	821081
3:	66	530	2571	83744	022481
4:	58	444	4409	50805	344316
5:	30	245	3913	01683	526897
6:	73	910	6755	00495	673063
7:	48	262	4867	49742	312302
8:	90	802	7132	85562	597766
9:	75	013	2520	51997	234537
10:	85	030	7194	98485	871332
11:	26	217	8393	57773	341156
12:	00	602	5589	69374	274072
13:	05	270	5394	05954	149256
14:	56	169	2815	51563	627863
15:	95	251	9547	36944	235812
16:	83	455	1373	22829	072025
17:	76	466	2219	20251	620972
18:	07	692	2188	92085	444670
19:	77	089	4465	24272	885736
20:	07	949	7922	32237	980455
21:	36	917	3474	01682	500573
22:	99	410	2564	02503	586462
23:	61	747	7966	43592	470434
24:	50	751	9465	12912	750889
25:	48	705	0425	22761	085242
26:	37	422	3041	09899	397052
27:	66	896	5657	37196	037571
28:	10	184	7859	77530	003016
29:	73	410	3022	63915	067665
30:	57	909	1398	01999	982944
31:	96	394	3939	23643	608452

JUNE	2-DIGIT	3-DIGIT	4-DIGIT	5-DIGIT	6-DIGIT
1:	00	125	9202	81670	757105
2:	83	796	5381	96793	710089
3:	60	263	9566	82928	459730
4:	82	442	5632	47479	126653
5:	01	255	7195	84685	121005
6:	22	136	8405	30414	654832
7:	85	938	2803	12791	859985
8:	94	531	6711	44724	637285
9:	61	812	4497	97861	074599
10:	63	994	5884	40955	713852
11:	07	270	3154	18687	979239
12:	01	353	3700	54134	572040
13:	05	659	8888	77284	829864
14:	32	122	3161	46977	697513
15:	31	979	4321	10657	410813
16:	83	356	7338	64044	491769
17:	64	055	9993	76401	994281
18:	30	456	5318	85497	811686
19:	16	652	9742	96104	249007
20:	74	754	9158	60155	825487
21:	78	019	4007	67119	621623
22:	69	694	9283	90896	130407
23:	60	638	0481	69249	034409
24:	50	837	7263	14982	292251
25:	62	549	1084	87065	161171
26:	34	720	0663	73826	595876
27:	29	683	2615	53315	808586
28:	50	975	4766	30045	373811
29:	62	717	7947	13419	824898
30:	62	392	4804	95035	440331

JULY	2-DIGIT	3-DIGIT	4-DIGIT	5-DIGIT	6-DIGIT
1:	98	275	4127	30169	047576
2:	36	452	3982	89575	085869
3:	57	359	3612	95910	038823
4:	17	248	6730	19313	828620
5:	33	683	3537	56389	372544
6:	62	917	3016	40270	019371
7:	93	247	0187	44097	073952
8:	26	104	3493	32861	612871
9:	41	489	3086	20634	873159
10:	37	067	1461	29727	473599
11:	94	506	3549	35939	483001
12:	33	008	6680	74773	757110
13:	98	907	1140	76964	189376
14:	77	925	5513	29852	607792
15:	60	939	1680	16364	234538
16:	27	733	9466	28724	329272
17:	58	438	0024	40081	723843
18:	20	802	4271	99367	976701
19:	87	429	9133	17118	481700
20:	61	603	3706	17936	054512
21:	84	136	9685	58771	274717
22:	10	456	5513	73263	686830
23:	80	834	2307	67308	351255
24:	51	441	4158	31357	631625
25:	11	555	1918	42464	191913
26:	59	145	7809	36629	240193
27:	51	774	5231	93404	732671
28:	55	519	2150	97483	049439
29:	08	802	5092	55765	009915
30:	17	890	8411	29730	796033
31:	12	158	4829	29788	805451

AUGUST	2-DIGIT	3-DIGIT	4-DIGIT	5-DIGIT	6-DIGIT
1:	58	117	0707	24333	053271
2:	06	506	3386	98422	407687
3:	84	509	5839	85184	678076
4:	20	821	2784	66806	636068
5:	84	544	2452	09527	688127
6:	37	023	9522	33428	574566
7:	58	445	9666	02626	503690
8:	99	527	4816	30168	899521
9:	14	876	4911	41647	915210
10:	80	764	8920	81104	255838
11:	68	538	9842	08525	675592
12:	85	455	9133	35562	007476
13:	32	649	3104	33369	565149
14:	17	100	1530	32425	144190
15:	36	756	6253	48419	511225
16:	51	568	0023	12096	770297
17:	12	582	9679	73641	442204
18:	86	270	8092	54633	695007
19:	95	253	5362	96852	301665
20:	30	486	4678	96788	393854
21:	33	050	5965	90959	324266
22:	44	695	9082	33426	548242
23:	74	944	6530	04633	417090
24:	23	117	8970	24018	057652
25:	85	720	7244	68997	962864
26:	63	562	5770	62415	106543
27:	21	036	6743	19940	201312
28:	25	240	6398	14985	598423
29:	42	232	6429	30979	399561
30:	75	241	9158	00933	168068
31:	37	496	4836	09402	866305

SEPTEMBER	2-DIGIT	3-DIGIT	4-DIGIT	5-DIGIT	6-DIGIT
1:	97	574	0068	25463	193799
2:	32	961	4227	74832	644797
3:	12	282	4397	97228	359349
4:	61	617	6285	92398	265909
5:	02	693	8399	97229	073300
6:	74	996	6398	44596	927133
7:	67	940	6015	65110	724486
8:	83	179	2119	46983	161803
9:	68	874	6994	50555	822404
10:	87	698	8581	92903	747697
11:	40	076	6491	67242	851224
12:	78	701	0212	23266	984872
13:	46	927	5212	36253	494882
14:	91	764	7702	54135	285992
15:	08	038	9001	18935	596557
16:	97	369	0776	14858	348699
17:	40	268	0042	02497	645483
18:	94	184	8317	49488	484218
19:	68	573	6454	22321	685643
20:	92	658	5871	02183	945975
21:	06	656	0318	26468	380713
22:	80	605	6824	29166	469146
23:	92	082	1498	87441	922744
24:	32	806	4127	73579	126614
25:	55	243	4601	40519	097117
26:	81	961	8305	09091	341177
27:	60	365	8625	21696	191221
28:	62	131	7075	04198	636037
29:	37	156	9114	16556	164874
30:	88	058	8631	23644	174348

OCTOBER	2-DIGIT	3-DIGIT	4-DIGIT	5-DIGIT	6-DIGIT
1:	76	728	9158	41711	405180
2:	07	973	4610	51686	110987
3:	36	729	8493	17242	155465
4:	34	338	9741	94092	315483
5:	68	103	9547	70193	873209
6:	01	408	5563	44781	350592
7:	70	005	4490	61657	092781
8:	04	575	4007	93091	747115
9:	71	369	5319	16114	607158
10:	84	186	4133	19944	550071
11:	36	498	0814	06827	007473
12:	59	242	9616	72891	543801
13:	43	659	7213	67809	378815
14:	88	460	8889	09527	105968
15:	07	250	2546	89768	999942
16:	80	713	7897	40894	694373
17:	19	395	7816	00431	617197
18:	30	250	7082	85438	072056
19:	23	853	5557	23769	144114
20:	56	551	3079	12415	050357
21:	75	870	5231	97043	935890
22:	59	658	6755	95851	003082
23:	92	297	5457	51121	487989
24:	72	501	8073	79037	036910
25:	71	452	0463	38070	922112
26:	98	757	7797	96851	005554
27:	97	334	7590	00930	158006
28:	01	966	6580	61347	863764
29:	44	380	6360	11849	031248
30:	79	490	6667	62980	581486
31:	62	688	8091	10216	149208

NOVEMBER	2-DIGIT	3-DIGIT	4-DIGIT	5-DIGIT	6-DIGIT
1:	50	960	3242	45036	162414
2:	43	159	0287	74961	920846
3:	98	851	3920	23701	200027
4:	39	084	2972	49992	791627
5:	00	774	3393	46413	206308
6:	52	358	7037	70444	378858
7:	06	880	4961	14172	045735
8:	23	760	5908	86255	078972
9:	54	583	0494	70881	768394
10:	94	220	4930	73832	494270
11:	85	669	3192	99489	624142
12:	66	664	3085	05829	761539
13:	68	160	6668	12661	705668
14:	46	036	3123	68187	986134
15:	72	425	5601	48923	279061
16:	86	467	9058	40457	886996
17:	60	934	4823	84430	848756
18:	45	073	1567	23388	336202
19:	92	009	1022	18559	433404
20:	66	237	0224	19248	582113
21:	81	519	8662	96227	790980
22:	63	883	2057	38319	105327
23:	85	471	6969	61844	272779
24:	31	595	2722	89766	841825
25:	23	607	0569	44910	626641
26:	55	575	4014	88131	827992
27:	72	148	1749	40139	272833
28:	79	344	0312	65298	740166
29:	62	548	5827	35245	001796
30:	65	438	9760	55888	223253

DECEMBER	2-DIGIT	3-DIGIT	4-DIGIT	5-DIGIT	6-DIGIT
1:	45	137	8198	77904	991789
2:	08	466	1366	13604	682460
3:	72	548	1184	97860	212592
4:	38	039	6699	40828	881969
5:	76	534	0846	36000	545067
6:	42	565	2144	40958	184342
7:	46	604	3506	60466	366878
8:	97	442	5733	94155	657397
9:	83	736	6165	82299	452231
10:	03	005	9522	49239	258417
11:	69	178	9265	09399	142292
12:	92	802	6046	09089	584639
13:	35	410	9440	21569	464807
14:	31	289	3712	21510	307334
15:	68	368	7559	03381	777176
16:	28	003	3248	06826	711363
17:	16	090	1473	66487	307952
18:	00	575	7828	38197	023781
19:	88	145	5111	77403	588974
20:	12	796	2683	37568	058869
21:	20	284	7018	27092	891397
22:	57	207	0501	87635	863142
23:	40	661	1548	16555	868763
24:	55	906	1542	17240	833031
25:	17	580	9516	00242	993034
26:	48	609	2207	34431	570838
27:	73	042	4120	50555	986721
28:	46	243	2533	90768	002314
29:	86	644	0030	90704	364389
30:	48	859	5268	82741	444050
31:	14	179	1925	48670	181191

JANUARY	2-DIGIT	3-DIGIT	4-DIGIT	5-DIGIT	6-DIGIT
1:	95	007	6128	61725	931510
2:	21	043	5168	55515	905845
3:	45	465	7157	66744	442209
4:	01	487	3851	45350	174294
5:	02	915	1310	54323	449727
6:	09	983	1780	65673	607208
7:	59	528	8236	34998	532533
8:	91	998	1755	43093	617253
9:	20	809	6943	91209	533805
10:	05	015	1391	96412	902067
11:	95	615	7508	89072	048246
12:	73	809	0626	80231	667408
13:	13	116	8048	85062	014371
14:	93	722	5005	28159	272170
15:	98	908	1699	95598	201323
16:	54	568	7916	85873	556998
17:	76	662	7270	35374	590217
18:	21	129	2307	28156	383839
19:	89	452	8323	97479	282839
20:	36	316	8707	07582	280958
21:	78	717	6993	49549	355642
22:	45	872	3775	92649	771558
23:	97	270	7797	56073	768443
24:	28	752	7816	58647	913324
25:	18	948	1448	42900	851234
26:	07	030	1730	94154	943446
27:	69	357	6053	30101	791007
28:	37	758	0852	81358	501763
29:	50	994	3543	17559	013091
30:	80	974	5068	23644	486721
31:	31	891	1925	75649	773444

FEBRUARY	2-DIGIT	3-DIGIT	4-DIGIT	5-DIGIT	6-DIGIT
1:	48	186	8311	90331	777195
2:	46	062	4013	28909	170572
3:	41	624	1523	82422	517514
4:	62	316	5444	83744	858164
5:	99	898	9402	52940	089598
6:	74	571	0375	78221	013732
7:	13	752	0645	41021	108415
8:	80	010	7100	26778	625993
9:	77	875	0406	60345	269071
10:	63	040	8995	59778	889534
11:	74	858	8336	21445	833627
12:	79	129	6749	82736	111553
13:	50	890	3443	06765	961669
14:	87	760	0087	56643	306097
15:	84	146	3694	92964	931494
16:	77	497	6836	83363	362514
17:	05	372	0369	15424	998022
18:	87	996	4654	49241	850638
19:	45	481	4497	11661	719458
20:	67	970	5871	57767	400176
21:	33	040	5940	75270	287857
22:	22	197	2382	15364	084011
23:	00	121	8261	30985	488596
24:	64	379	6824	42965	219473
25:	96	164	2540	14799	609068
26:	48	469	5858	40709	540700
27:	76	087	3292	01749	609087
28:	76	423	7678	62792	999910
29:	92	622	3343	17684	713181

MARCH	2-DIGIT	3-DIGIT	4-DIGIT	5-DIGIT	6-DIGIT
1:	71	616	9811	13608	136688
2:	73	912	5601	89701	621642
3:	45	944	8831	82740	131678
4:	33	952	8901	02876	861284
5:	82	423	6197	41083	424005
6:	01	142	1636	40891	223884
7:	81	167	7464	48106	229558
8:	44	161	5049	34869	092167
9:	45	777	7225	08207	521857
10:	96	668	6718	10153	494922
11:	37	777	0287	87754	204411
12:	49	107	9102	50806	910212
13:	22	942	6009	05953	017463
14:	72	668	9679	43024	646731
15:	18	735	3700	30794	288475
16:	43	403	3707	50179	225148
17:	49	264	0124	01563	471677
18:	60	085	8035	14046	970389
19:	16	873	1730	03695	476684
20:	16	531	1247	40394	814868
21:	04	952	1102	70189	418981
22:	00	150	1147	52939	941544
23:	52	995	1303	30292	843073
24:	36	158	5952	26215	430898
25:	31	405	1266	15989	472965
26:	29	648	6002	28971	798534
27:	32	878	8028	52877	435312
28:	99	711	0733	09774	009334
29:	89	887	8455	98294	115376
30:	61	969	1436	08773	753338
31:	62	275	7250	00556	274701

APRIL	2-DIGIT	3-DIGIT	4-DIGIT	5-DIGIT	6-DIGIT
1:	60	134	7226	12852	297306
2:	52	633	6128	08774	319235
3:	55	078	9346	94279	765266
4:	54	668	1159	64733	222636
5:	98	215	4352	97040	883242
6:	01	551	0482	99866	829881
7:	18	371	1655	38821	698784
8:	04	293	2740	44285	237688
9:	16	942	6272	79598	623522
10:	03	648	0545	30227	056994
11:	77	797	2119	59776	445369
12:	30	130	2175	77659	427120
13:	80	556	1617	48864	973534
14:	01	971	2778	63852	291647
15:	44	079	5821	83616	894487
16:	83	450	2903	72260	674296
17:	28	267	1918	69442	678697
18:	25	540	7596	62100	798552
19:	19	128	7677	44721	436582
20:	71	024	8098	43401	836209
21:	22	473	7389	24396	141661
22:	99	457	1988	62599	921519
23:	09	616	4051	74835	802914
24:	70	388	0670	93212	532549
25:	35	543	9033	04698	055114
26:	60	902	3732	42528	872523
27:	19	506	0588	03068	255723
28:	62	050	4321	31734	673047
29:	04	717	6535	88137	874440
30:	39	710	0343	34242	153579

MAY	2-DIGIT	3-DIGIT	4-DIGIT	5-DIGIT	6-DIGIT
1:	25	327	2878	79291	013049
2:	04	257	0212	49239	110362
3:	47	602	0193	61470	007102
4:	26	312	1354	94282	801653
5:	85	700	2552	10780	206310
6:	83	062	9308	00683	836798
7:	38	101	6592	96480	428422
8:	42	961	4591	05701	781600
9:	26	742	4233	82045	206306
10:	10	654	5821	40205	815450
11:	63	659	3330	31864	663048
12:	93	560	7226	56262	376343
13:	72	423	5701	59718	435951
14:	79	680	4039	07459	173089
15:	07	785	3054	67115	585237
16:	38	663	7890	44848	146734
17:	76	897	6580	76152	080853
18:	02	287	1153	28915	799179
19:	38	959	8148	30732	078354
20:	23	376	9170	36066	627258
21:	35	077	3067	03255	511189
22:	89	964	1981	28408	767757
23:	45	954	2840	06386	893923
24:	10	098	1279	12977	431500
25:	18	066	4258	89200	070771
26:	38	698	2132	58776	337428
27:	15	094	0042	17303	757103
28:	52	092	3110	66554	146680
29:	28	042	7935	00620	077043
30:	63	346	6950	28033	424024
31:	29	096	2401	62974	683093

JUNE	2-DIGIT	3-DIGIT	4-DIGIT	5-DIGIT	6-DIGIT
1:	67	428	6937	44845	110348
2:	45	760	5187	30104	097179
3:	17	440	6197	25271	740153
4:	90	410	2038	34118	479813
5:	98	787	7289	69185	544441
6:	23	628	1573	54947	542570
7:	94	358	2433	78348	575829
8:	85	943	0055	15297	287869
9:	94	230	6172	16490	500525
10:	66	772	0733	07142	167408
11:	29	573	8656	00181	243341
12:	20	279	0821	24587	463514
13:	57	508	1040	05321	999902
14:	35	701	5312	96728	775954
15:	78	326	7715	68560	303542
16:	15	677	1849	94343	403291
17:	02	453	5921	83243	142976
18:	32	001	8751	31110	146100
19:	00	039	7978	69185	396385
20:	01	052	2502	07018	371911
21:	28	763	7740	63542	898312
22:	35	233	3167	04508	029372
23:	46	003	1768	95664	029989
24:	36	505	0821	00240	713186
25:	53	427	1053	88510	313579
26:	19	037	2527	29598	361867
27:	68	587	9033	07330	897040
28:	21	215	3531	40642	744558
29:	70	196	1203	87254	621016
30:	67	816	0532	26968	947845

JULY	2-DIGIT	3-DIGIT	4-DIGIT	5-DIGIT	6-DIGIT
1:	04	461	3192	08024	690618
2:	60	013	3474	05320	703792
3:	02	549	7169	00871	434636
4:	46	242	7276	38948	843039
5:	16	362	9127	72766	991766
6:	07	999	6058	31043	201903
7:	72	572	7872	17308	237655
8:	27	851	0663	56388	642330
9:	22	462	8023	38135	274088
10:	49	816	2671	67559	587118
11:	96	262	9604	92335	072050
12:	09	636	9798	33052	664938
13:	50	889	7131	54944	802294
14:	07	478	8129	28158	828004
15:	43	180	5538	51812	689347
16:	45	995	2784	52001	418978
17:	27	637	7659	92461	025664
18:	78	553	8041	65676	077698
19:	87	861	8587	76776	025641
20:	87	087	2734	83115	597141
21:	98	780	4220	96225	050704
22:	76	898	7753	98675	357502
23:	33	814	1397	98360	779725
24:	83	255	9334	25276	760278
25:	84	471	7495	30230	379428
26:	94	555	3399	64173	767818
27:	50	624	8461	02875	729491
28:	09	922	3060	43091	337404
29:	24	627	4735	45288	276546
30:	52	010	9798	86003	277212
31:	16	959	2953	05634	837403

AUGUST	2-DIGIT	3-DIGIT	4-DIGIT	5-DIGIT	6-DIGIT
1:	82	259	0275	75961	028787
2:	03	888	6053	84058	870044
3:	57	548	0425	32302	618480
4:	84	702	8236	20192	315444
5:	33	090	6963	26027	849322
6:	60	339	5463	12911	036937
7:	45	326	0312	81109	424017
8:	72	175	5426	52565	745866
9:	47	713	9936	34809	802902
10:	09	356	6880	92086	010566
11:	69	892	6561	17995	376302
12:	95	707	1900	85312	954124
13:	06	390	2307	93280	371277
14:	63	011	9139	56574	213844
15:	35	997	4515	82611	707574
16:	36	806	0306	28474	849946
17:	48	467	3763	68683	220770
18:	53	457	9754	80910	832379
19:	66	578	1366	01431	307297
20:	65	060	6191	89454	316696
21:	30	154	4779	67810	674926
22:	20	612	5977	05385	341817
23:	50	334	1931	08834	354976
24:	80	028	0619	62471	105898
25:	15	849	6623	42084	558270
26:	90	679	6906	99240	980500
27:	96	041	1818	36565	898280
28:	46	141	8612	81298	153649
29:	54	817	9246	93025	247083
30:	08	629	1373	08024	960405
31:	19	664	7427	13733	958510

SEPTEMBER	2-DIGIT	3-DIGIT	4-DIGIT	5-DIGIT	6-DIGIT
1:	48	924	5984	66555	982363
2:	68	391	3982	92208	927794
3:	07	673	3411	04571	910859
4:	59	833	7345	14047	118445
5:	38	449	0802	51623	647342
6:	83	126	5939	55200	492385
7:	54	557	7991	91525	677479
8:	48	377	5551	73766	412080
9:	82	157	2270	37193	297295
10:	23	199	4610	37886	360660
11:	20	647	8505	00430	469142
12:	19	674	8010	37509	902397
13:	57	364	0865	08963	361239
14:	07	947	6190	91080	691860
15:	38	748	9772	76216	570822
16:	28	496	6843	88950	548860
17:	06	151	6799	39449	558227
18:	72	259	0833	94596	935264
19:	81	531	8455	40079	819250
20:	83	272	6015	51311	974158
21:	79	098	1077	19624	475479
22:	53	105	5262	83425	408318
23:	77	853	9898	31673	341195
24:	46	614	8173	13540	192491
25:	46	444	5494	27278	462912
26:	70	848	8048	32111	296627
27:	26	651	9183	77470	237061
28:	96	111	5701	04134	981750
29:	52	402	9472	48109	265945
30:	64	298	6441	80917	075841

OCTOBER	2-DIGIT	3-DIGIT	4-DIGIT	5-DIGIT	6-DIGIT
1:	23	531	0984	56201	208809
2:	73	972	1291	93533	008719
3:	41	089	1673	23957	890118
4:	75	269	2834	02812	641101
5:	15	865	4459	78914	929041
6:	89	519	6523	55636	151707
7:	02	442	1912	49050	380730
8:	66	960	6373	21010	470416
9:	75	396	9917	21068	749619
10:	75	391	2006	99680	258367
11:	94	836	5162	94345	265298
12:	27	408	5105	72823	869390
13:	64	843	1059	03251	474803
14:	58	932	0589	82360	784083
15:	61	107	7884	13289	834897
16:	62	443	4114	16363	938428
17:	83	582	1322	32866	093423
18:	26	354	0639	10468	368809
19:	31	488	0494	67243	565176
20:	91	080	0325	75465	646095
21:	00	279	2828	04134	146068
22:	11	947	3424	45975	415193
23:	20	866	9980	04380	589006
24:	01	887	8292	60778	040062
25:	01	470	9540	29731	674303
26:	74	188	9949	79852	721392
27:	74	529	5175	91332	329302
28:	16	720	3361	33052	237096
29:	69	662	5162	09150	376919
30:	85	210	9898	89889	637321
31:	23	312	2539	81549	971670

NOVEMBER	2-DIGIT	3-DIGIT	4-DIGIT	5-DIGIT	6-DIGIT
1:	18	473	0714	88136	430275
2:	84	982	4183	90456	747072
3:	52	843	8192	11469	667391
4:	69	676	0770	23457	471041
5:	52	629	8217	76840	827983
6:	84	417	1448	99490	772197
7:	87	240	1103	53758	826729
8:	45	649	1360	27468	488654
9:	95	641	8957	78975	139162
10:	20	652	0005	69750	749598
11:	16	734	8970	47358	341218
12:	36	081	3481	96101	673048
13:	46	420	8807	07829	332379
14:	81	930	3029	16550	536266
15:	91	723	2006	75334	508040
16:	90	755	4120	77533	578975
17:	12	639	3374	16240	560773
18:	53	998	2376	42021	068301
19:	74	471	1216	28659	125350
20:	29	850	4221	27848	312938
21:	97	258	6950	12221	740174
22:	18	469	2803	56201	939023
23:	14	321	7339	85121	754002
24:	86	415	9190	00494	376952
25:	16	110	6724	43338	076453
26:	47	718	7747	55949	242732
27:	76	698	9798	30420	823012
28:	89	575	7332	56831	930259
29:	66	788	7514	43971	538180
30:	28	413	8274	56578	520017

DECEMBER	2-DIGIT	3-DIGIT	4-DIGIT	5-DIGIT	6-DIGIT
1:	28	607	6586	62288	274660
2:	89	194	3380	27252	767140
3:	56	346	3787	01810	210726
4:	93	176	1046	24707	936575
5:	41	561	1730	48111	022483
6:	89	147	5626	81044	907724
7:	62	466	5544	83991	909585
8:	02	111	5438	19942	375692
9:	20	422	8606	60906	750214
10:	06	237	8023	51935	918947
11:	54	897	3713	84371	273442
12:	12	925	1335	59465	486136
13:	30	481	8481	94282	071439
14:	34	351	6504	08646	461027
15:	39	735	2847	24146	349964
16:	08	365	2703	55954	887602
17:	10	108	1303	18119	467909
18:	39	669	0959	17809	640471
19:	23	521	0400	32424	265921
20:	74	831	1134	08903	595283
21:	41	647	8869	31299	605945
22:	33	135	7847	22327	748254
23:	07	295	0400	46224	016249
24:	78	913	2176	25714	281607
25:	56	311	0601	87882	914564
26:	43	874	6529	83557	154856
27:	01	757	8718	99925	569512
28:	10	170	5839	11156	803566
29:	32	496	8819	92024	112818
30:	19	092	5049	49675	203788
31:	03	684	3073	25273	184320

JANUARY	2-DIGIT	3-DIGIT	4-DIGIT	5-DIGIT	6-DIGIT
1:	49	361	7188	79099	934659
2:	21	357	1975	06390	094627
3:	90	780	6624	56890	669890
4:	48	481	1698	05759	642962
5:	45	511	3298	04317	395147
6:	17	830	9691	96601	526229
7:	77	363	1329	40079	549463
8:	24	620	2063	42899	824910
9:	23	530	8594	96162	856845
10:	82	947	9152	34498	843670
11:	08	706	3186	08708	654886
12:	33	687	1448	88323	863796
13:	33	472	0914	35059	012440
14:	70	676	9189	55072	364391
15:	90	669	7539	12980	007458
16:	46	400	3556	41525	563879
17:	34	787	3110	98798	317316
18:	93	170	7320	32865	379471
19:	12	975	9471	58270	707584
20:	66	240	2878	99362	913990
21:	72	792	4603	73078	411426
22:	99	346	2904	18689	153618
23:	07	535	5908	00054	829299
24:	59	664	0482	87693	454718
25:	10	883	6661	30415	802887
26:	96	514	1874	60720	030644
27:	60	020	1404	48983	420272
28:	11	417	0331	08650	227627
29:	11	115	0287	61782	184389
30:	37	538	4121	25588	327992
31:	87	499	2357	55258	501802

FEBRUARY	2-DIGIT	3-DIGIT	4-DIGIT	5-DIGIT	6-DIGIT
1:	94	418	1153	00930	740164
2:	20	738	3556	15553	543856
3:	22	217	8129	73580	840565
4:	69	622	4723	82170	863810
5:	46	314	6975	66425	992363
6:	79	548	4347	24083	425891
7:	74	959	8054	89642	628487
8:	41	674	6630	62476	856236
9:	49	260	8129	40331	203168
10:	40	774	0532	60218	585242
11:	53	774	4704	25019	626021
12:	82	559	1473	23076	228915
13:	80	784	7200	87253	907065
14:	64	437	0419	74770	286621
15:	70	679	1843	35185	696268
16:	80	942	3480	89830	627904
17:	82	967	4403	11349	717640
18:	56	850	3104	37008	873836
19:	20	240	6134	30792	992364
20:	10	252	5563	54322	883830
21:	16	179	9685	71950	011174
22:	60	770	5312	81923	558865
23:	21	419	2922	51494	641080
24:	56	208	0368	26591	906423
25:	31	764	4842	57393	664926
26:	20	560	5613	84057	843720
27:	83	048	7288	34309	531880
28:	97	186	2389	14042	473576
29:	04	039	9296	53377	002444

MARCH	2-DIGIT	3-DIGIT	4-DIGIT	5-DIGIT	6-DIGIT
1:	31	116	9993	73769	152355
2:	80	142	5519	87384	939651
3:	75	962	9127	01371	853714
4:	69	988	1893	64920	656157
5:	47	810	1084	52189	148610
6:	08	279	1479	43468	526881
7:	28	365	8424	28344	235202
8:	08	169	8079	98423	973583
9:	76	312	7935	89453	168641
10:	08	578	6762	19881	504267
11:	54	017	1285	90578	664299
12:	01	624	6097	98045	201948
13:	32	801	6216	41645	740831
14:	85	688	6711	35183	104048
15:	14	533	8248	87569	050738
16:	96	799	4578	52124	796634
17:	57	220	6605	83307	945318
18:	40	437	7464	36939	215688
19:	89	393	4860	26718	172410
20:	71	803	6109	35811	503063
21:	90	696	5300	44157	257749
22:	73	524	3838	59529	124161
23:	68	265	3242	12792	991778
24:	78	031	9848	42716	723886
25:	38	223	0344	93464	916467
26:	92	045	3550	13605	560730
27:	35	578	6304	47923	128534
28:	59	854	7853	32172	046321
29:	55	981	1624	97861	238917
30:	22	540	9836	38820	968569
31:	63	944	6692	42150	492405

APRIL	2-DIGIT	3-DIGIT	4-DIGIT	5-DIGIT	6-DIGIT
1:	62	396	1661	26969	826114
2:	97	851	4578	53130	263396
3:	10	940	0356	73014	921456
4:	73	242	6159	48108	403937
5:	39	343	7257	80790	243957
6:	99	782	8819	29163	146711
7:	75	430	1272	93591	600296
8:	12	206	7841	37817	824242
9:	27	876	3167	46292	838714
10:	58	305	6347	27655	356278
11:	52	434	4648	29856	913965
12:	40	621	8079	60277	472929
13:	57	149	6906	45282	795994
14:	77	251	2245	85622	781563
15:	22	539	3920	68118	745827
16:	12	700	7351	90643	884483
17:	68	181	7834	60215	696911
18:	44	319	1328	37447	707538
19:	74	307	2264	44786	952875
20:	82	839	7979	11975	567021
21:	77	180	2941	39263	674340
22:	78	497	0262	93779	181872
23:	72	377	2589	40895	260270
24:	11	198	8857	94154	213232
25:	29	008	0005	38513	045724
26:	93	432	4390	04821	120397
27:	20	258	9654	77033	577739
28:	48	226	1780	36062	173030
29:	44	819	8650	00866	102140
30:	82	954	8794	97042	623517

MAY	2-DIGIT	3-DIGIT	4-DIGIT	5-DIGIT	6-DIGIT
1:	76	255	0814	36438	336183
2:	74	950	9202	96476	974195
3:	51	703	0174	03312	372552
4:	19	732	1046	50680	956598
5:	53	131	6711	73329	604702
6:	23	696	9277	21192	423385
7:	38	127	9095	75837	519338
8:	89	804	3970	95220	863790
9:	18	255	5155	44342	533153
10:	53	013	4296	08148	216330
11:	11	172	0437	44095	794104
12:	31	922	1284	86940	355613
13:	87	484	1492	99678	353774
14:	47	306	6906	46289	262756
15:	30	971	7050	85876	863170
16:	55	344	2615	79287	828608
17:	62	650	9747	55262	956030
18:	96	265	0544	53567	340559
19:	28	053	7301	86880	050084
20:	13	988	5212	33620	652956
21:	41	450	7903	45475	413957
22:	67	348	9441	34748	201264
23:	92	602	3511	19623	179369
24:	20	953	7119	87568	172469
25:	33	769	0513	02060	880692
26:	46	299	4396	91963	780966
27:	50	990	5632	85625	521839
28:	10	418	7169	18309	493651
29:	54	463	1868	64674	483005
30:	16	521	0168	35251	778458
31:	83	454	4402	52127	954751

JUNE	2-DIGIT	3-DIGIT	4-DIGIT	5-DIGIT	6-DIGIT
1:	56	509	7878	25527	265927
2:	89	943	6893	89073	074570
3:	58	310	4817	78223	754008
4:	00	632	4949	80665	856240
5:	22	773	2671	00809	224515
6:	15	215	3794	24834	350617
7:	02	176	2069	74458	031278
8:	36	878	0005	55951	999270
9:	01	653	8982	20000	654895
10:	21	312	0695	28972	364431
11:	25	576	0124	57146	925878
12:	87	469	3656	62849	983003
13:	59	360	7288	89893	986080
14:	24	570	6956	73391	380720
15:	36	526	4854	39575	511841
16:	41	071	9076	27220	453494
17:	29	398	8856	61910	042596
18:	53	880	0620	95721	743295
19:	44	803	0814	74583	731369
20:	83	114	9176	40646	346841
21:	83	030	4691	37572	095255
22:	51	316	8411	73140	875071
23:	42	054	5457	80732	816699
24:	87	210	7658	13169	467304
25:	79	496	3424	84120	915848
26:	29	030	1009	48550	961653
27:	43	215	1755	95038	762766
28:	33	053	7960	41644	592775
29:	63	112	7640	87255	933389
30:	38	043	3556	72762	373221

JULY	2-DIGIT	3-DIGIT	4-DIGIT	5-DIGIT	6-DIGIT
1:	97	936	5243	46981	717637
2:	14	041	0833	06769	310428
3:	88	019	3449	48484	609677
4:	91	051	6881	24329	181202
5:	34	020	5946	50239	678731
6:	45	336	4421	15549	237684
7:	43	535	1730	29667	602175
8:	28	206	6228	65611	291619
9:	28	501	4754	20884	934643
10:	76	811	4698	44785	656765
11:	49	688	9835	05571	331172
12:	34	096	2502	09651	213837
13:	89	182	7540	72202	664878
14:	87	923	3782	88695	424666
15:	51	769	9033	80352	304787
16:	56	820	2690	15170	186200
17:	03	842	8857	35938	917105
18:	41	311	4584	70504	266545
19:	10	255	8217	34436	215707
20:	07	452	6680	48801	631620
21:	96	338	6159	51746	607157
22:	42	482	1862	89704	092131
23:	84	277	9183	24519	624785
24:	30	041	0934	42898	841172
25:	60	499	3474	46098	046372
26:	72	026	7998	43154	679318
27:	29	260	2408	57394	961037
28:	53	712	3757	79914	079568
29:	16	132	7728	53375	992382
30:	97	501	5111	46166	885101
31:	89	493	8104	05577	838048

AUGUST	2-DIGIT	3-DIGIT	4-DIGIT	5-DIGIT	6-DIGIT
1:	54	405	8964	02000	279054
2:	29	546	1027	19501	844300
3:	01	051	7244	55198	318005
4:	48	481	5783	35057	420220
5:	94	372	3957	63357	787225
6:	04	501	7715	53755	086453
7:	58	770	7056	77277	740829
8:	43	984	4440	04944	646108
9:	72	312	6617	05261	668051
10:	77	599	5896	32678	094005
11:	85	061	1811	61596	507406
12:	24	897	6573	70566	894507
13:	11	509	4723	94343	133505
14:	43	802	1969	74831	888259
15:	87	327	5212	07648	632934
16:	29	881	2922	20257	937206
17:	33	905	5789	84054	685603
18:	15	941	1015	38325	464148
19:	23	260	8587	12289	684370
20:	35	936	2909	18625	097752
21:	88	523	8123	35750	483584
22:	92	715	8907	25901	001176
23:	02	422	7220	90834	518708
24:	96	459	9911	59278	200671
25:	03	567	0821	97608	976729
26:	92	113	1254	79850	441544
27:	78	347	2966	45412	072043
28:	63	821	1768	12096	622241
29:	90	006	0607	25712	271545
30:	10	780	3399	39826	017490
31:	46	543	8474	86063	043168

SEPTEMBER	2-DIGIT	3-DIGIT	4-DIGIT	5-DIGIT	6-DIGIT
1:	82	519	8004	77345	727612
2:	92	027	3618	15296	870028
3:	13	003	3148	70697	180618
4:	44	609	2502	68873	976726
5:	19	600	6711	29918	525666
6:	04	905	8650	80795	306668
7:	14	419	4403	73203	216985
8:	47	687	2075	92838	501190
9:	89	912	1617	07080	269660
10:	78	668	8198	31862	070826
11:	27	256	1994	64547	799177
12:	96	255	5877	00493	514946
13:	80	156	7539	53758	244570
14:	16	876	4384	83809	808561
15:	17	804	7188	17244	435313
16:	30	520	1949	40013	467274
17:	32	108	1141	80602	498064
18:	80	065	0118	28220	455966
19:	34	434	2044	11720	712612
20:	81	344	8072	78031	570149
21:	17	626	6712	48363	945973
22:	64	952	8047	96229	922774
23:	48	384	5193	36311	086458
24:	73	987	2815	67994	220116
25:	60	646	0388	62415	794170
26:	40	809	3719	74146	775936
27:	03	077	8167	76716	302272
28:	32	363	4484	60716	576416
29:	59	762	6987	57141	011222
30:	94	407	7144	66737	977919

OCTOBER	2-DIGIT	3-DIGIT	4-DIGIT	5-DIGIT	6-DIGIT
1:	29	621	1667	08210	262133
2:	83	548	1022	60343	137278
3:	89	540	4804	61785	802934
4:	98	447	2489	15295	991759
5:	50	078	9083	20633	264676
6:	23	688	0293	77529	706905
7:	40	259	5933	68057	831816
8:	24	825	0958	72386	627910
9:	97	079	0162	91519	196927
10:	73	513	7997	83932	021899
11:	88	737	2182	99678	205718
12:	36	730	7834	98360	092097
13:	53	482	2358	71070	080185
14:	06	634	5726	68498	675580
15:	14	423	5344	34435	485494
16:	66	998	0632	46666	886337
17:	52	011	9698	75209	225791
18:	13	641	7972	49179	656779
19:	52	424	5896	47483	311094
20:	43	863	6604	78662	275337
21:	73	472	8054	48864	391375
22:	72	198	5801	20193	611554
23:	66	242	4051	21884	190639
24:	03	424	5902	42523	391972
25:	44	641	3035	02687	835542
26:	68	629	4233	94218	581470
27:	18	142	0814	48611	711346
28:	71	544	4196	04882	764622
29:	59	482	1040	86877	579594
30:	74	654	5915	81295	265318
31:	45	361	6925	94906	434068

NOVEMBER	2-DIGIT	3-DIGIT	4-DIGIT	5-DIGIT	6-DIGIT
1:	77	221	8800	45033	422138
2:	56	280	5984	24771	278490
3:	46	194	8348	60217	706974
4:	91	849	9585	85502	710080
5:	72	638	0319	31733	064564
6:	90	338	6423	35939	213216
7:	84	462	2728	66361	502393
8:	53	339	7602	53501	676210
9:	06	767	9402	70378	148613
10:	92	792	4967	03947	548229
11:	13	806	2740	03507	895107
12:	56	466	5444	37315	378841
13:	20	631	5413	22328	044465
14:	40	447	7489	52628	252098
15:	11	997	1561	44780	636641
16:	56	626	4378	20006	431558
17:	39	328	6391	25210	095929
18:	62	186	9597	13727	477957
19:	73	358	3154	23952	557622
20:	12	085	3298	60907	316110
21:	87	040	9064	56204	514981
22:	52	655	6636	37446	247110
23:	82	504	0168	40516	356841
24:	94	082	5055	58900	593352
25:	07	602	4108	58212	698167
26:	24	790	3687	29161	554490
27:	98	021	6040	01876	023129
28:	37	038	8016	89139	008705
29:	28	247	6667	92591	910196
30:	77	396	7677	44348	579602

DECEMBER	2-DIGIT	3-DIGIT	4-DIGIT	5-DIGIT	6-DIGIT
1:	17	083	7219	16806	644199
2:	08	029	4892	84495	677421
3:	27	115	3418	37756	492390
4:	69	774	3750	71695	156766
5:	65	040	1498	20690	560142
6:	61	654	8317	06078	405181
7:	48	677	6881	81925	568927
8:	67	950	0124	99550	538153
9:	54	539	9478	13538	018112
10:	50	262	3286	81357	205653
11:	17	843	6454	11155	671773
12:	48	890	4628	94032	131687
13:	31	577	9202	54072	361919
14:	74	632	5407	52623	337442
15:	28	935	6103	59215	737025
16:	50	858	8267	25019	208180
17:	12	332	8449	77282	803539
18:	58	516	8970	48984	716382
19:	44	569	8474	04507	568945
20:	54	200	9672	91394	539423
21:	37	853	6843	47165	844986
22:	83	848	2220	07458	337406
23:	56	331	7006	75527	839954
24:	94	231	1429	68311	659900
25:	35	055	1636	35626	540032
26:	70	434	7866	41333	485488
27:	51	887	4873	55949	407049
28:	35	243	3750	28285	077729
29:	45	144	0870	80294	443425
30:	26	052	3625	92898	102827
31:	96	560	4986	79542	206326

JANUARY	2-DIGIT	3-DIGIT	4-DIGIT	5-DIGIT	6-DIGIT
1:	18	387	9490	75650	069554
2:	02	238	2358	00681	514364
3:	21	449	6367	92083	000504
4:	22	361	8305	69939	479229
5:	98	376	2790	87819	842435
6:	87	892	3863	69316	830551
7:	56	728	9353	29476	280322
8:	71	156	7175	22889	213235
9:	02	416	3493	88444	067072
10:	68	873	7652	69437	780304
11:	69	554	7019	15925	982995
12:	03	545	0313	68936	048854
13:	65	687	0432	44159	849970
14:	39	934	9070	51244	701327
15:	43	434	3066	61470	807315
16:	66	661	6347	96417	546936
17:	29	131	9014	87318	693144
18:	23	798	4252	41209	272150
19:	70	954	9879	73515	636644
20:	29	034	7865	69937	347436
21:	13	770	9653	89826	755835
22:	10	482	6962	63166	883214
23:	27	677	1686	56827	433445
24:	43	954	5080	93653	958472
25:	54	914	0394	10406	592791
26:	07	658	4917	48860	476719
27:	89	136	0344	24082	711939
28:	71	580	7941	37444	967262
29:	76	427	7960	94595	205051
30:	40	077	3462	37944	073967
31:	29	840	9553	74774	592793

FEBRUARY	2-DIGIT	3-DIGIT	4-DIGIT	5-DIGIT	6-DIGIT
1:	05	435	4246	89580	270310
2:	99	966	4077	89887	193155
3:	69	584	6379	27216	565163
4:	20	942	6535	63791	124113
5:	34	628	0356	17431	467256
6:	46	858	1592	88758	496793
7:	07	751	1699	94592	734561
8:	01	848	3110	96165	580859
9:	43	751	7520	24205	507436
10:	71	285	9911	74083	417760
11:	60	368	5614	14674	639191
12:	52	582	1680	58148	938412
13:	39	036	4045	71261	550092
14:	85	261	3850	59149	924622
15:	17	997	1279	71134	136050
16:	24	646	3512	32803	915826
17:	70	372	6918	96228	939036
18:	85	459	0074	96794	170517
19:	52	066	1661	76651	055765
20:	81	200	8555	00554	100321
21:	60	834	6028	65737	097177
22:	86	737	3926	95032	282214
23:	58	189	0407	51810	097125
24:	69	691	8606	49739	841812
25:	51	469	7835	43783	104658
26:	79	924	1542	11975	254648
27:	07	953	9917	93469	248964
28:	56	228	2031	55510	885720
29:	62	509	0645	70632	542594

MARCH	2-DIGIT	3-DIGIT	4-DIGIT	5-DIGIT	6-DIGIT
1:	30	504	5168	13731	096502
2:	33	162	1523	24206	221388
3:	74	664	0024	15735	078984
4:	15	721	3229	72008	290377
5:	61	765	7401	49988	173082
6:	50	864	5024	56706	542542
7:	89	674	1366	05069	615984
8:	78	199	0795	87821	164870
9:	15	650	5143	63166	153000
10:	75	223	5639	65239	582693
11:	99	522	8619	17116	577106
12:	25	072	5450	69880	051970
13:	76	804	1629	71824	163028
14:	91	958	7069	49299	146104
15:	73	552	2521	29663	417733
16:	86	494	6818	71634	137287
17:	77	164	5105	02434	303569
18:	89	551	1699	37383	905196
19:	67	871	3550	28410	777819
20:	92	485	1097	54442	790996
21:	08	429	9334	10470	543188
22:	26	564	2702	13164	716966
23:	45	980	1918	85874	270950
24:	79	935	7382	87572	356910
25:	86	482	9923	96037	035024
26:	98	636	4045	99866	517509
27:	47	144	9685	93027	273408
28:	82	130	4509	06016	941536
29:	06	074	4328	09336	800378
30:	87	274	8374	96983	900148
31:	33	708	5482	27658	556982

APRIL	2-DIGIT	3-DIGIT	4-DIGIT	5-DIGIT	6-DIGIT
1:	54	999	1717	23139	004933
2:	93	614	2778	05636	995521
3:	66	381	0400	26153	115308
4:	10	273	6730	01875	875074
5:	15	462	8945	41210	838047
6:	62	757	1975	77785	232679
7:	28	792	1843	23012	321104
8:	83	348	8487	81425	732008
9:	74	083	3537	27784	510596
10:	00	928	8236	06393	670586
11:	28	009	5921	09215	162998
12:	44	570	3731	56328	622851
13:	23	587	1630	19879	912046
14:	78	713	6053	98864	087133
15:	15	455	6272	38821	280942
16:	33	171	9716	87944	812312
17:	93	779	8041	41330	327371
18:	83	780	7545	59964	339318
19:	61	423	1003	15985	288523
20:	76	041	5538	34994	644202
21:	81	542	8380	44974	698769
22:	01	557	7734	02372	257765
23:	17	070	2170	21134	562023
24:	08	358	8976	53565	330497
25:	92	522	0099	38825	153011
26:	05	657	7157	36126	646737
27:	33	952	9459	21511	767762
28:	60	066	8600	97104	373210
29:	27	760	6172	59901	579562
30:	86	563	0306	58085	284125

MAY	2-DIGIT	3-DIGIT	4-DIGIT	5-DIGIT	6-DIGIT
1:	74	617	3487	97043	083945
2:	80	234	5827	43779	068272
3:	58	787	0149	65927	165506
4:	22	106	4961	89826	295407
5:	18	679	5921	58897	392649
6:	28	919	7709	03752	459777
7:	84	375	6247	12602	087767
8:	91	313	3819	45788	965410
9:	34	301	8368	09840	239579
10:	03	976	8449	08520	507413
11:	70	818	4604	91522	937202
12:	60	392	2301	23576	664255
13:	41	499	6698	63162	698773
14:	74	964	1222	62850	279113
15:	92	617	5432	85750	327398
16:	57	654	7395	03004	841223
17:	36	841	7577	71699	923366
18:	36	525	8939	68873	289098
19:	90	827	9735	75712	845572
20:	26	068	6880	19064	602820
21:	23	287	6347	43466	934661
22:	63	061	4246	36629	658035
23:	32	001	8255	39198	052578
24:	77	682	1436	35752	345591
25:	28	670	8092	26028	833059
26:	33	264	0582	62974	952879
27:	55	247	1466	72453	588368
28:	52	622	6203	03879	439715
29:	26	793	7627	43218	587129
30:	26	696	1122	73770	030624
31:	43	067	0639	37447	855593

JUNE	2-DIGIT	3-DIGIT	4-DIGIT	5-DIGIT	6-DIGIT
1:	09	993	1146	51933	474781
2:	99	169	6498	30038	866934
3:	03	352	6203	15046	348117
4:	81	561	8870	51370	401417
5:	01	669	2238	46166	154887
6:	48	039	2056	03443	092765
7:	60	029	6730	31486	203784
8:	30	276	8530	64795	268440
9:	70	696	4936	13288	226414
10:	59	064	4001	74712	277203
11:	18	334	3707	64985	336768
12:	07	171	4917	08082	134139
13:	19	659	9515	81798	467257
14:	87	562	2809	18998	954733
15:	39	077	3330	87447	117248
16:	20	944	1793	15611	283488
17:	14	910	2314	45916	945348
18:	87	719	9747	40457	738941
19:	39	358	5751	36501	678097
20:	79	583	6875	19129	553216
21:	42	299	4133	07770	174908
22:	19	010	5821	98421	111577
23:	41	357	8751	89326	442227
24:	77	737	3399	37194	175565
25:	85	229	8675	77403	276602
26:	41	568	9660	91774	738962
27:	98	121	8788	88823	595245
28:	37	339	8556	17372	145466
29:	24	287	0432	72764	817387
30:	11	817	4905	85122	050113

JULY	2-DIGIT	3-DIGIT	4-DIGIT	5-DIGIT	6-DIGIT
1:	52	934	6668	37008	455995
2:	50	118	3110	84998	672457
3:	88	089	7332	16053	693148
4:	96	311	7740	01687	293498
5:	44	396	3141	38131	402019
6:	77	435	6285	19376	858162
7:	57	088	8186	22701	631659
8:	31	350	8744	95913	631044
9:	83	551	1962	21575	405787
10:	09	851	3361	15614	188081
11:	61	441	9515	93971	842421
12:	84	050	7803	27403	850629
13:	47	856	4195	60465	218823
14:	86	866	6661	46227	486738
15:	06	141	1473	67493	774714
16:	53	400	2634	38451	999920
17:	21	950	4861	88572	777224
18:	62	640	5080	02188	130417
19:	48	263	0783	20444	535045
20:	41	941	6473	37069	205688
21:	79	342	4496	05389	674313
22:	04	517	1467	61286	679967
23:	08	854	6015	95728	519958
24:	52	714	6511	70822	462867
25:	21	618	8650	97227	898921
26:	68	814	4189	98675	775343
27:	03	041	4421	44154	099632
28:	05	418	7565	63545	950960
29:	04	339	0495	00492	202573
30:	10	929	4515	97417	924663
31:	94	713	6153	45540	617878

AUGUST	2-DIGIT	3-DIGIT	4-DIGIT	5-DIGIT	6-DIGIT
1:	15	813	3537	38951	418998
2:	44	696	8424	14544	484874
3:	03	088	8092	81611	287260
4:	50	648	5149	22323	860023
5:	98	839	8079	58651	097766
6:	60	661	1912	36877	005567
7:	69	366	1379	12604	769988
8:	67	617	9051	37503	542575
9:	09	575	8192	69065	055116
10:	02	605	4948	62221	435931
11:	61	727	3274	85376	608410
12:	81	250	3004	51180	375675
13:	76	876	1329	99301	312352
14:	55	144	1234	00616	580228
15:	40	512	3461	88262	844316
16:	45	597	4522	16803	755867
17:	99	573	2571	86376	864407
18:	08	757	4208	59465	216351
19:	71	829	4528	96417	816722
20:	88	677	2966	85183	947861
21:	69	472	6736	64672	890785
22:	40	218	5990	32990	201292
23:	97	286	4578	92902	139214
24:	27	697	6379	25590	190000
25:	12	454	1542	55385	333685
26:	26	743	9490	33866	365681
27:	90	936	6724	58143	293543
28:	05	520	2540	73015	905195
29:	35	167	1279	98171	319879
30:	50	264	9466	72134	408309
31:	89	228	0651	80477	840560

SEPTEMBER	2-DIGIT	3-DIGIT	4-DIGIT	5-DIGIT	6-DIGIT
1:	89	963	5011	57706	660482
2:	94	710	3499	65426	286001
3:	07	663	9302	70131	991723
4:	88	578	9986	36945	262136
5:	56	061	4509	20821	158625
6:	64	981	9121	26401	568309
7:	46	743	9854	64735	397016
8:	04	397	6560	42961	035031
9:	54	557	2075	20822	454736
10:	96	133	6209	22259	804157
11:	79	828	0294	94347	857519
12:	04	711	0337	75085	446556
13:	50	011	0883	62476	290339
14:	57	562	7088	36061	712602
15:	52	016	6554	07143	611574
16:	83	301	5871	43967	649848
17:	18	958	5953	58458	601533
18:	06	428	0651	48234	669925
19:	78	382	8524	69755	082094
20:	80	917	8506	89264	560740
21:	64	907	7822	18811	087108
22:	82	285	8694	36567	342445
23:	01	869	4773	25084	560156
24:	63	496	4378	37444	385103
25:	46	549	0984	40389	630426
26:	62	240	1693	76213	264649
27:	49	814	1498	45036	310470
28:	65	735	8305	22890	091504
29:	64	446	8612	38508	877545
30:	89	794	9861	60780	050123

OCTOBER	2-DIGIT	3-DIGIT	4-DIGIT	5-DIGIT	6-DIGIT
1:	89	377	1109	19186	684365
2:	21	719	7150	27907	618466
3:	71	860	3230	88826	335522
4:	24	218	1805	57016	893290
5:	76	944	4948	36248	310441
6:	49	157	7238	49611	131660
7:	57	702	9352	11032	860014
8:	10	109	7778	07456	597130
9:	68	451	2702	25337	092130
10:	42	573	6912	94280	061377
11:	98	820	8248	60590	458485
12:	41	299	4792	26652	238275
13:	00	866	3204	21443	241406
14:	13	826	1517	91021	534387
15:	75	722	3619	58087	040663
16:	88	131	3587	02941	377578
17:	93	238	5024	99110	260286
18:	56	744	6134	66306	651093
19:	69	101	6793	79285	384442
20:	07	922	3587	00929	444054
21:	87	587	5412	09148	202539
22:	90	133	7690	43968	380062
23:	70	307	0946	60593	346816
24:	51	860	7113	24771	156759
25:	08	119	3468	10281	517446
26:	01	770	0739	66299	874431
27:	51	085	1096	93594	758413
28:	70	312	4114	44348	891974
29:	01	802	5914	48045	627920
30:	26	513	1680	72954	155501
31:	96	838	8838	77780	212555

NOVEMBER	2-DIGIT	3-DIGIT	4-DIGIT	5-DIGIT	6-DIGIT
1:	51	033	0732	61719	154847
2:	03	132	9472	59276	174346
3:	19	960	7684	99616	890129
4:	05	703	4353	84247	599675
5:	49	296	5300	72762	225166
6:	35	513	9673	93407	472947
7:	43	398	6454	37127	797264
8:	60	565	0664	19249	608437
9:	55	125	1799	94219	877580
10:	51	294	7903	44469	947195
11:	14	628	4635	34494	225125
12:	58	797	4817	19001	991119
13:	70	109	4722	22948	100921
14:	05	791	6749	08708	237045
15:	52	565	8424	31982	438420
16:	11	309	2684	96790	821758
17:	50	807	7245	84809	646715
18:	74	189	5368	69189	850613
19:	03	311	6918	98860	780961
20:	35	773	9873	94907	042552
21:	93	756	2276	71384	345589
22:	86	966	5820	95789	269651
23:	91	043	8951	80666	570191
24:	36	152	2784	42460	885740
25:	80	462	2464	92715	001803
26:	11	359	7791	76845	160479
27:	48	706	0984	41395	991719
28:	15	065	6498	76467	240788
29:	82	619	1247	45658	393250
30:	15	580	0701	87509	163051

DECEMBER	2-DIGIT	3-DIGIT	4-DIGIT	5-DIGIT	6-DIGIT
1:	75	981	7903	88885	492994
2:	87	244	9014	75145	317981
3:	16	310	9259	32803	481723
4:	62	070	9014	89950	535070
5:	73	217	4052	39322	144185
6:	21	644	0494	68249	031938
7:	44	801	5130	65172	622235
8:	44	085	2577	04756	334317
9:	61	897	5821	10594	486740
10:	48	951	3744	97732	232654
11:	85	621	4265	20759	382608
12:	40	151	3543	08018	479853
13:	33	799	9873	13351	568328
14:	64	697	1674	86818	856225
15:	19	931	6611	58896	244593
16:	17	343	9692	55823	289118
17:	07	886	1555	97796	304782
18:	41	603	6931	34999	706913
19:	86	179	3964	89014	769043
20:	73	814	8537	01619	158659
21:	84	777	5946	79850	007440
22:	70	150	4007	39134	668078
23:	51	473	4691	65171	595910
24:	60	479	9440	06764	247717
25:	73	381	8919	04444	539403
26:	19	794	6078	25082	280308
27:	68	314	2170	91523	233313
28:	93	544	9390	29980	005572
29:	84	583	7138	92774	159275
30:	73	279	3944	94974	690638
31:	88	966	4239	27404	163002

JANUARY	2-DIGIT	3-DIGIT	4-DIGIT	5-DIGIT	6-DIGIT
1:	50	966	9999	66176	496776
2:	21	501	2150	02748	733291
3:	18	535	4691	62538	753985
4:	99	165	9641	08650	375682
5:	32	797	9359	20257	249578
6:	14	027	8813	40395	110978
7:	37	104	9246	76594	760299
8:	43	234	1586	82552	402046
9:	51	310	5080	62416	254598
10:	32	612	4760	67868	266502
11:	91	834	1090	29791	275940
12:	91	836	3318	52314	552589
13:	23	468	3562	21759	533135
14:	67	658	4748	16303	215059
15:	28	858	3073	10467	072699
16:	87	336	3405	71385	223858
17:	48	891	0940	45852	185593
18:	01	964	0105	72010	734543
19:	15	493	3562	04321	579589
20:	60	437	0156	90578	680562
21:	38	699	0977	47982	286006
22:	22	880	5062	50301	576479
23:	05	241	4879	83869	410199
24:	35	558	0557	79160	266511
25:	79	459	1392	70440	776576
26:	83	046	1473	63854	466027
27:	39	261	8029	29537	151746
28:	37	455	4496	93216	299149
29:	07	029	6473	42334	784071
30:	89	075	5150	12163	418383
31:	96	897	1642	40207	259616

FEBRUARY	2-DIGIT	3-DIGIT	4-DIGIT	5-DIGIT	6-DIGIT
1:	00	090	1931	38445	789155
2:	95	737	1260	96603	536292
3:	23	893	9585	88135	552006
4:	22	952	0118	40393	831130
5:	42	028	7038	20126	503040
6:	89	229	9993	61596	777192
7:	73	548	0526	78978	149224
8:	67	077	8261	17806	752139
9:	14	065	7025	34305	347438
10:	55	579	1925	20065	319243
11:	42	703	9648	45474	265902
12:	46	772	0369	86820	136074
13:	15	113	8819	15364	396383
14:	70	348	1285	76779	913972
15:	86	542	5055	81234	515625
16:	16	032	4484	85061	326744
17:	63	843	8029	73953	697546
18:	20	071	9930	33867	392005
19:	64	542	9860	56136	274674
20:	92	036	8386	79165	747063
21:	64	218	8945	70821	166756
22:	77	466	1561	01370	557603
23:	36	730	3750	69063	314840
24:	15	726	1699	22577	688107
25:	09	069	7702	11344	115357
26:	43	910	9616	86690	294128
27:	47	740	8255	84621	065139
28:	03	124	0620	66110	414586
29:	18	989	1228	40452	406444

MARCH	2-DIGIT	3-DIGIT	4-DIGIT	5-DIGIT	6-DIGIT
1:	18	765	7144	71382	753368
2:	10	663	0588	93527	692485
3:	15	875	9127	31988	649186
4:	37	522	6285	88759	957221
5:	89	554	3794	98862	225127
6:	90	501	7088	49240	554527
7:	02	329	6353	15803	483609
8:	35	886	5431	38701	939673
9:	34	725	2163	53693	876332
10:	27	743	3575	63163	142938
11:	29	692	7382	17183	685620
12:	01	191	0564	30169	465417
13:	06	574	7006	45916	405776
14:	79	522	1843	34179	229506
15:	27	116	8675	89576	651765
16:	38	162	5708	00180	529389
17:	06	900	9653	72388	802289
18:	92	261	2370	37440	348717
19:	26	518	9591	94341	541284
20:	77	498	6736	83116	311093
21:	01	159	5388	48423	711929
22:	41	251	6423	66556	008687
23:	53	997	7119	00747	908926
24:	94	083	0313	10720	752727
25:	88	989	5011	76150	070790
26:	66	757	2897	80859	796637
27:	40	628	0093	33238	966665
28:	14	878	0726	12102	981062
29:	38	795	2225	65610	577667
30:	25	122	4641	68686	273418
31:	11	564	6027	76903	005580

APRIL	2-DIGIT	3-DIGIT	4-DIGIT	5-DIGIT	6-DIGIT
1:	03	373	7370	62600	233892
2:	79	843	7075	20629	228290
3:	92	551	8901	31481	734232
4:	55	412	0977	74961	772790
5:	76	275	4848	75773	029369
6:	62	595	8280	35186	114110
7:	50	063	6504	35624	947811
8:	04	131	2633	49618	908322
9:	76	718	5049	07271	591512
10:	36	719	7251	74584	149210
11:	54	341	2200	86440	772217
12:	05	193	2922	75841	391407
13:	60	184	1410	43403	592747
14:	58	428	6573	24523	973544
15:	31	299	4296	45287	250222
16:	78	509	6661	88011	190612
17:	29	444	6052	10030	995535
18:	69	223	6461	57519	200699
19:	08	145	1887	60340	936574
20:	99	752	9459	17872	564543
21:	57	927	3995	98736	525036
22:	43	265	6862	64545	206957
23:	31	952	0644	98231	937780
24:	05	988	7715	94533	429033
25:	17	247	7885	19561	985511
26:	26	001	8518	23391	658637
27:	09	662	1247	12409	755853
28:	86	732	6510	55010	884484
29:	10	991	9051	90454	154841
30:	86	540	2959	19755	090225

MAY	2-DIGIT	3-DIGIT	4-DIGIT	5-DIGIT	6-DIGIT
1:	61	874	5049	61848	578951
2:	11	277	8067	33679	080215
3:	53	022	9064	61469	093364
4:	63	282	6235	44219	885711
5:	64	779	1398	19437	041958
6:	04	615	8531	38822	142949
7:	58	126	8901	88071	644195
8:	25	621	1404	24017	761542
9:	52	568	0156	73140	727015
10:	20	478	6385	32803	751509
11:	21	721	2966	98362	684318
12:	29	785	7590	73332	657351
13:	81	802	5550	27723	491117
14:	13	053	1843	88136	308544
15:	47	907	9302	40520	663013
16:	73	764	0400	02813	937212
17:	48	017	1548	74771	164890
18:	32	604	5908	85249	612210
19:	01	757	5689	70627	792255
20:	61	309	5180	62663	411488
21:	35	825	0796	34870	552595
22:	38	580	9321	12477	012422
23:	84	426	9641	63228	363121
24:	07	355	9120	79352	180584
25:	13	708	5676	15424	432125
26:	95	299	2558	44972	254603
27:	46	829	0519	58586	851258
28:	08	497	7038	76715	424003
29:	70	333	9365	10652	765944
30:	49	841	5833	65798	846871
31:	14	960	6366	15423	284070

JUNE	2-DIGIT	3-DIGIT	4-DIGIT	5-DIGIT	6-DIGIT
1:	48	195	7163	72950	536956
2:	46	033	0469	88073	653257
3:	72	152	8606	72073	658615
4:	50	004	8211	70633	838704
5:	28	976	4829	56767	292235
6:	18	003	2752	25460	617840
7:	94	627	4930	33054	257158
8:	15	193	2364	57206	379460
9:	83	646	7953	87382	643541
10:	31	810	2038	05513	617865
11:	36	903	1454	35308	195655
12:	48	495	8361	20066	737084
13:	13	930	1617	91268	691278
14:	68	935	8600	25088	326757
15:	35	981	0764	85627	114059
16:	86	722	2401	20570	070817
17:	40	631	1692	13352	298542
18:	05	151	6667	88952	601508
19:	64	257	3072	35434	731428
20:	46	080	3581	96349	724470
21:	39	634	3788	74831	618472
22:	28	781	1260	99236	378217
23:	73	207	9384	96795	318572
24:	73	642	0733	24579	120955
25:	47	794	4303	15360	777839
26:	10	439	1862	76525	250206
27:	33	964	9384	26406	752750
28:	89	351	0319	58711	551348
29:	55	733	6209	61411	771574
30:	41	816	5074	28225	206304

JULY	2-DIGIT	3-DIGIT	4-DIGIT	5-DIGIT	6-DIGIT
1:	41	329	4152	37943	925911
2:	17	264	0482	26845	422135
3:	83	767	2496	64292	257143
4:	71	647	5086	95601	941599
5:	42	553	2220	36063	304823
6:	18	319	1786	98858	188740
7:	69	469	5695	01392	465385
8:	17	588	2452	12160	530052
9:	87	336	9321	42088	446602
10:	99	135	0281	97359	793515
11:	15	294	2081	14856	174319
12:	45	086	7834	56576	388224
13:	41	179	6724	28532	859364
14:	89	811	1899	38883	474801
15:	27	228	8317	52121	326144
16:	29	886	6253	30981	452210
17:	43	348	5431	96917	235799
18:	11	422	7583	11155	655511
19:	10	920	9748	44095	942159
20:	42	498	0356	34869	526270
21:	53	079	6184	14484	031291
22:	97	910	3794	57078	521253
23:	78	198	1454	06703	228238
24:	86	506	2527	86188	282830
25:	48	691	8405	56387	780323
26:	86	508	8838	38008	442205
27:	18	079	0363	84872	258415
28:	27	474	6993	79160	684352
29:	60	581	4415	26781	201951
30:	05	209	0758	02123	762178
31:	59	129	9973	99799	869422

AUGUST	2-DIGIT	3-DIGIT	4-DIGIT	5-DIGIT	6-DIGIT
1:	15	531	2828	98232	921517
2:	67	912	2834	44596	344974
3:	38	168	9039	10904	149862
4:	05	343	0350	74705	352486
5:	89	742	8938	20818	540080
6:	03	072	0752	36694	904542
7:	84	060	3129	09906	634142
8:	77	715	2395	27157	259636
9:	35	446	1310	97733	528764
10:	28	773	1353	16616	618456
11:	83	235	2928	37631	834886
12:	33	114	2596	45475	979854
13:	60	151	0482	28471	797298
14:	80	360	7489	72698	047569
15:	79	531	5952	79166	043174
16:	97	370	6034	66678	508074
17:	20	550	0946	30982	018106
18:	35	045	7527	90640	726365
19:	00	075	0507	64230	629180
20:	80	393	8581	25147	918333
21:	06	099	6931	99486	048184
22:	38	330	2734	53503	268431
23:	82	071	4635	72640	725779
24:	67	960	4791	52625	363766
25:	02	436	9240	57208	823626
26:	37	374	4114	31169	155517
27:	41	383	6115	39385	755885
28:	75	823	2119	78220	865677
29:	91	071	1573	93092	043225
30:	14	521	2407	11971	948476
31:	27	270	3518	39009	010574

SEPTEMBER	2-DIGIT	3-DIGIT	4-DIGIT	5-DIGIT	6-DIGIT
1:	08	459	8694	21761	125356
2:	43	067	9980	08018	792225
3:	14	026	2897	69692	888235
4:	86	860	9905	25086	152377
5:	40	799	8555	39706	962269
6:	33	717	0808	99614	445963
7:	50	870	8192	29914	193168
8:	40	617	0168	38890	087146
9:	86	594	9007	50494	802925
10:	99	717	2188	74647	491124
11:	59	974	9873	98546	351239
12:	06	895	6881	69752	193764
13:	71	462	5130	91144	747725
14:	46	654	7558	40520	811068
15:	84	340	8417	50742	002402
16:	25	612	6241	89577	947876
17:	82	314	2797	96038	870707
18:	49	984	0093	02001	262792
19:	92	576	6147	69564	760242
20:	22	972	8399	46542	482357
21:	38	927	6560	96918	114068
22:	74	347	1648	61219	571453
23:	21	841	0902	35439	211979
24:	32	944	1134	96730	220120
25:	33	054	3876	12347	710049
26:	14	250	6981	38762	541311
27:	51	373	5532	15608	707529
28:	76	682	1962	93590	452240
29:	90	630	8769	89888	653584
30:	61	282	8474	31486	055729

OCTOBER	2-DIGIT	3-DIGIT	4-DIGIT	5-DIGIT	6-DIGIT
1:	34	730	5331	26901	421490
2:	77	686	2376	86437	614100
3:	47	087	5594	79856	218206
4:	97	363	7608	41650	803541
5:	89	325	1241	79223	174321
6:	76	790	0105	86815	951632
7:	73	400	8355	10840	242051
8:	08	012	1636	68876	177429
9:	99	388	2056	73832	764056
10:	34	321	7144	97355	878860
11:	22	232	5569	29291	274704
12:	39	424	1724	72136	270316
13:	14	183	9836	80604	672444
14:	86	247	2326	74140	713226
15:	88	439	2638	32676	231998
16:	60	106	2627	61469	780991
17:	93	161	3211	98425	565804
18:	42	615	2112	81168	745807
19:	84	747	6586	68559	425273
20:	42	647	7784	44280	487349
21:	81	532	4767	91899	873156
22:	53	554	6918	69249	452251
23:	20	064	0287	71322	717627
24:	84	712	9315	25334	351854
25:	54	694	2608	54636	313552
26:	45	057	3731	97106	965431
27:	93	064	1404	62163	156728
28:	61	731	0130	06763	099662
29:	62	806	0902	56516	474214
30:	53	304	0331	10276	602791
31:	18	709	5281	80735	974816

NOVEMBER	2-DIGIT	3-DIGIT	4-DIGIT	5-DIGIT	6-DIGIT
1:	73	528	5833	10214	392670
2:	87	682	1799	56074	376925
3:	42	131	7928	10845	574548
4:	72	195	0118	10782	502420
5:	27	213	7452	96541	178115
6:	81	185	7031	26092	783456
7:	41	276	8368	27278	193125
8:	22	196	3041	34246	041910
9:	71	977	5645	54007	723895
10:	36	848	0645	44660	417102
11:	83	149	1705	25145	474167
12:	51	371	0771	55700	641676
13:	28	651	7602	09085	130411
14:	33	151	5024	29727	055757
15:	24	279	1580	90145	057626
16:	11	845	8449	36504	566428
17:	88	039	9196	06701	471700
18:	61	551	3342	86061	450947
19:	17	849	5042	84246	451621
20:	28	720	6228	24833	054508
21:	69	024	3926	78600	795429
22:	93	794	9566	26338	644236
23:	12	338	5205	98423	137901
24:	25	963	1887	87318	423358
25:	64	252	9245	43344	122902
26:	14	280	6341	50053	123479
27:	69	876	2809	21010	888257
28:	45	623	2941	77409	069526
29:	97	555	1291	37949	554519
30:	14	705	7107	64608	982974

DECEMBER	2-DIGIT	3-DIGIT	4-DIGIT	5-DIGIT	6-DIGIT
1:	75	669	6780	47422	413346
2:	92	063	6147	10342	102822
3:	81	449	9227	88825	727039
4:	21	945	1693	15364	232066
5:	11	697	6278	78914	659255
6:	40	974	2571	57771	896990
7:	46	874	8374	25588	867565
8:	95	696	0262	61535	011236
9:	07	249	3204	08650	063310
10:	62	570	6335	63917	929672
11:	81	864	0582	02126	814827
12:	28	236	7301	95784	937154
13:	27	755	9415	38761	245201
14:	08	221	8443	19751	471680
15:	43	598	2577	63978	991738
16:	91	315	4992	68311	242059
17:	65	933	8612	79286	220125
18:	48	271	9635	03064	189337
19:	31	018	2929	85686	689373
20:	19	870	2634	84494	920884
21:	02	160	4233	37629	660507
22:	37	932	0387	99554	722595
23:	06	146	8888	18062	172444
24:	01	599	2935	89260	942195
25:	14	997	9453	29104	423342
26:	20	706	1968	71192	579571
27:	73	188	0607	98733	784760
28:	55	385	2558	14355	459132
29:	78	189	6128	34747	444725
30:	67	647	4227	30043	347486
31:	88	217	3756	15427	738297

JANUARY	2-DIGIT	3-DIGIT	4-DIGIT	5-DIGIT	6-DIGIT
1:	37	850	1159	37754	630383
2:	44	819	4566	71568	324883
3:	33	198	8135	48550	231439
4:	91	866	6762	92903	017483
5:	89	622	1498	65107	105941
6:	33	270	3751	46729	498037
7:	06	190	0268	95727	059530
8:	70	016	4415	66552	972301
9:	22	860	5726	54699	925252
10:	09	341	5356	07077	799170
11:	50	334	8901	79536	577719
12:	31	167	9961	13979	713820
13:	18	179	8600	95477	998047
14:	20	167	1178	51495	789135
15:	78	784	9440	74520	077082
16:	08	359	9534	72199	342444
17:	59	165	2502	94845	996748
18:	31	275	1692	55136	002416
19:	27	454	2301	20943	927798
20:	80	080	6899	65049	826738
21:	33	274	0607	78663	883820
22:	87	851	8167	90516	052599
23:	37	445	4472	88074	262740
24:	85	425	9773	23271	319840
25:	15	252	6881	27968	489889
26:	48	159	0551	59154	526905
27:	29	831	3731	10905	610289
28:	97	146	1391	78974	843052
29:	77	395	2916	73893	513749
30:	73	650	9585	17746	880715
31:	37	766	9704	63977	261523

FEBRUARY	2-DIGIT	3-DIGIT	4-DIGIT	5-DIGIT	6-DIGIT
1:	80	914	5852	09150	228863
2:	63	634	0826	41960	466663
3:	57	717	7847	66743	294153
4:	80	911	4779	97421	109105
5:	36	321	5563	39516	772210
6:	59	272	4892	54884	348711
7:	11	301	3832	14171	061997
8:	60	836	0789	36192	163030
9:	33	662	8286	79538	604043
10:	15	773	4152	11971	800421
11:	05	695	5501	91080	839915
12:	49	324	8844	24145	636012
13:	95	986	1535	03756	226377
14:	55	861	3688	60785	816724
15:	20	381	5237	15422	405801
16:	11	693	9422	46980	273472
17:	59	313	4673	52436	903921
18:	79	445	9371	04066	471657
19:	42	131	7270	91963	511180
20:	01	339	1680	87759	372590
21:	54	745	3631	94846	980486
22:	94	200	6812	05199	918357
23:	48	269	3455	12287	092150
24:	70	527	8732	16363	520587
25:	13	354	8298	76525	668047
26:	04	191	2408	72200	072657
27:	11	619	8550	96980	847500
28:	75	601	9208	31673	489250
29:	57	190	6190	61469	363150

MARCH	2-DIGIT	3-DIGIT	4-DIGIT	5-DIGIT	6-DIGIT
1:	74	878	3587	98297	707597
2:	37	273	5613	11035	330504
3:	38	443	7075	59781	090238
4:	65	540	4735	65359	177487
5:	20	650	4189	09842	683745
6:	58	703	5609	62853	019389
7:	79	497	8681	35941	075223
8:	09	417	1912	66488	334277
9:	84	181	0965	36189	004913
10:	75	555	2013	83553	536312
11:	41	847	0350	10218	011215
12:	47	486	0168	56328	040692
13:	04	814	4654	65673	337422
14:	00	876	4283	37132	277816
15:	35	324	8217	19630	104087
16:	49	545	1887	31735	969157
17:	37	868	4679	83995	215758
18:	82	794	0783	63855	614082
19:	61	837	7101	77465	322405
20:	13	050	0244	08023	976667
21:	56	634	2307	63669	042568
22:	37	202	9553	32989	783451
23:	26	059	2609	47108	713838
24:	04	534	8148	87321	999317
25:	03	481	9597	85122	510541
26:	10	370	8374	00621	208836
27:	47	847	0086	26025	405156
28:	06	506	9302	69124	630430
29:	35	753	5181	36691	285998
30:	23	255	4760	09652	075844
31:	14	031	6724	61782	496761

APRIL	2-DIGIT	3-DIGIT	4-DIGIT	5-DIGIT	6-DIGIT
1:	21	522	6184	42083	426477
2:	17	073	3769	01248	893900
3:	09	631	5971	30415	950942
4:	17	090	0946	08648	201303
5:	26	615	7151	63790	097789
6:	61	022	7219	19438	486124
7:	58	343	4691	93155	549456
8:	68	700	4033	32489	782215
9:	74	541	1015	66930	431564
10:	95	249	4422	46167	033156
11:	11	069	7176	53506	008707
12:	70	950	8939	12283	368136
13:	09	723	0363	26656	962289
14:	50	776	2628	21697	905173
15:	76	404	8242	45849	297262
16:	02	403	7784	73891	921528
17:	97	241	4353	15484	393549
18:	61	598	9879	15299	445986
19:	51	336	3500	12475	568257
20:	30	698	3480	19441	956614
21:	97	676	3988	34934	042564
22:	64	789	5011	72511	867572
23:	52	617	8292	71945	948463
24:	56	132	0783	37882	488591
25:	49	162	1065	52248	740186
26:	79	501	6592	57328	461006
27:	80	972	9811	71824	432815
28:	51	609	1021	57711	400821
29:	28	120	5005	53125	930899
30:	46	757	1874	31109	701935

MAY	2-DIGIT	3-DIGIT	4-DIGIT	5-DIGIT	6-DIGIT
1:	92	880	8418	28408	185598
2:	16	076	5864	62727	213830
3:	32	261	9509	51245	727651
4:	27	934	6203	59463	893916
5:	54	177	3248	92020	494273
6:	58	183	6680	59968	645490
7:	40	105	6347	70445	526914
8:	17	456	4033	62100	110925
9:	89	355	0601	90515	756489
10:	04	293	6328	81670	026891
11:	42	341	9333	94659	964806
12:	15	937	3104	06391	078364
13:	52	705	0688	06953	585832
14:	69	402	3907	97103	807314
15:	35	957	5131	66178	089996
16:	87	910	7383	05010	310457
17:	94	703	5570	21763	569522
18:	98	795	6141	62351	304201
19:	13	600	6974	03564	026256
20:	35	885	9516	67999	822399
21:	72	481	2822	02186	268410
22:	23	308	1598	20317	703162
23:	10	205	3110	54381	876986
24:	20	554	2941	92214	286615
25:	55	462	6084	44468	216981
26:	63	174	8587	32359	479842
27:	04	471	8355	42464	504285
28:	30	372	0833	82423	665569
29:	73	937	3461	31673	923354
30:	65	387	5149	67746	872584
31:	23	176	7263	89009	166760

JUNE	2-DIGIT	3-DIGIT	4-DIGIT	5-DIGIT	6-DIGIT
1:	31	439	1699	39009	280360
2:	74	464	8543	36816	673715
3:	00	264	1962	38007	998039
4:	63	246	3148	41086	746439
5:	18	795	1862	45288	546332
6:	11	661	3750	83868	531929
7:	72	528	6492	39643	350569
8:	69	538	9183	89643	612224
9:	04	599	0695	12540	772178
10:	70	181	0338	31674	367519
11:	20	115	1310	11532	279091
12:	33	854	2395	33428	304780
13:	99	899	5714	04760	248973
14:	54	853	1278	06706	386355
15:	54	613	9854	82172	456031
16:	12	617	2207	68687	569528
17:	65	716	4171	72761	241428
18:	73	589	4553	43343	557005
19:	32	477	5300	56330	632913
20:	70	118	8831	67935	914588
21:	75	045	4108	85810	093353
22:	33	954	4716	73331	927137
23:	40	454	0557	25589	745834
24:	58	621	5381	11599	821709
25:	17	170	4358	99994	227661
26:	41	016	7113	25778	623521
27:	61	944	8273	99988	599054
28:	45	576	0488	77468	062681
29:	01	929	3493	47666	724491
30:	98	397	7878	27153	641091

JULY	2-DIGIT	3-DIGIT	4-DIGIT	5-DIGIT	6-DIGIT
1:	68	789	6329	56704	368162
2:	83	597	9158	59148	358725
3:	25	194	9202	66865	645485
4:	25	888	0588	79728	047627
5:	11	794	8085	04629	962862
6:	21	858	4553	32176	648603
7:	78	815	4057	37632	818625
8:	95	039	7715	95539	895795
9:	70	072	2690	19815	961650
10:	59	807	8267	34559	741418
11:	59	506	3643	77028	827401
12:	14	710	0275	48362	528132
13:	94	725	6078	39888	497398
14:	25	221	6962	08589	895775
15:	53	119	0871	97732	502440
16:	44	272	8217	18624	637325
17:	96	720	7082	31481	993018
18:	04	063	4929	72826	027508
19:	32	949	8386	99235	648004
20:	33	753	3336	94660	573289
21:	19	316	3217	58589	739589
22:	17	952	9359	74835	237018
23:	78	585	9629	99490	936515
24:	36	785	6109	51623	081446
25:	01	323	4899	50930	001819
26:	55	905	5068	38450	703810
27:	88	799	6717	92715	435907
28:	29	556	5695	72575	669914
29:	49	948	7006	88320	123519
30:	46	592	7665	84868	370084
31:	18	913	4672	91587	871338

AUGUST	2-DIGIT	3-DIGIT	4-DIGIT	5-DIGIT	6-DIGIT
1:	71	059	0012	34559	593363
2:	37	930	5626	29099	656742
3:	48	221	4528	33556	850615
4:	44	014	9189	29099	238900
5:	78	994	2559	77215	425239
6:	22	851	0959	90831	048218
7:	58	126	9559	06953	707563
8:	06	477	8788	47039	891372
9:	14	036	2922	74834	924645
10:	07	464	6605	53696	616608
11:	14	622	6824	13354	890764
12:	81	455	1899	80667	178674
13:	39	425	2897	94659	546965
14:	45	710	0080	60597	652989
15:	30	542	2458	68685	395150
16:	49	534	1963	26840	089638
17:	19	583	2960	22387	932151
18:	43	821	0745	72892	527539
19:	05	583	2332	17873	294757
20:	98	381	0043	00871	270319
21:	87	591	3324	41083	693791
22:	60	688	5588	49303	478600
23:	36	735	1002	71568	742724
24:	04	425	1159	94344	551346
25:	14	029	4993	31171	208166
26:	09	490	3443	45916	823617
27:	49	749	4867	90520	654882
28:	49	279	6905	27845	842448
29:	58	030	7652	70443	247065
30:	22	380	1824	16179	959135
31:	36	350	9007	80105	131635

SEPTEMBER	2-DIGIT	3-DIGIT	4-DIGIT	5-DIGIT	6-DIGIT
1:	33	218	2828	06766	987993
2:	61	366	3223	54635	287228
3:	61	557	0595	99113	878831
4:	06	654	4503	56013	314860
5:	32	679	2464	44660	147316
6:	35	604	7753	27280	219450
7:	95	697	7232	32238	128511
8:	58	943	2546	60157	565763
9:	65	899	8311	06763	369448
10:	11	457	4855	54381	728930
11:	98	873	3869	44285	115957
12:	78	972	0337	29662	539464
13:	24	569	1699	21571	221345
14:	56	243	2897	21637	139217
15:	00	105	9867	75521	211347
16:	97	896	4804	20001	099060
17:	75	145	6855	83305	770938
18:	34	255	5256	91018	063898
19:	36	494	3267	05761	547556
20:	92	041	1554	52373	397690
21:	15	161	7746	94095	637918
22:	95	861	9773	64043	195658
23:	31	903	1849	80544	652964
24:	98	371	5934	55884	456652
25:	16	337	5965	63981	732013
26:	89	300	9296	07954	989883
27:	17	590	4183	53317	713179
28:	96	506	3023	67553	376352
29:	70	048	6003	00366	831117
30:	70	890	3248	18999	981057

OCTOBER	2-DIGIT	3-DIGIT	4-DIGIT	5-DIGIT	6-DIGIT
1:	45	317	4986	09153	535036
2:	43	316	7226	85873	705053
3:	98	238	6341	83302	760876
4:	87	724	7000	42962	061356
5:	38	057	5212	18815	541336
6:	84	543	3110	28409	751494
7:	08	879	7960	56450	704396
8:	21	913	2433	04320	701320
9:	97	513	5036	40514	764620
10:	17	778	9823	56638	016186
11:	32	434	4284	98987	882630
12:	26	161	7188	75460	731440
13:	18	218	7370	08022	246453
14:	05	285	7314	61534	197285
15:	93	870	3092	56452	296616
16:	97	323	7665	96035	278486
17:	73	681	4861	99739	685626
18:	16	408	6323	10339	944705
19:	23	342	1899	92840	553838
20:	47	019	7890	03064	337392
21:	53	594	0946	33615	860032
22:	85	464	7326	99300	598400
23:	51	765	1122	58964	919004
24:	85	159	5846	20381	193131
25:	36	413	8800	24963	626666
26:	88	745	1592	00932	871957
27:	04	344	6692	13545	524988
28:	09	627	3976	79730	787902
29:	98	673	2389	54820	710687
30:	63	516	9070	95661	141658
31:	26	050	7445	02121	900171

NOVEMBER	2-DIGIT	3-DIGIT	4-DIGIT	5-DIGIT	6-DIGIT
1:	07	826	7696	45916	257721
2:	57	946	2771	86250	058848
3:	61	521	3982	74770	868780
4:	99	452	8819	89392	270892
5:	58	673	5249	51562	331753
6:	62	994	2458	30539	894495
7:	40	371	0933	93217	716991
8:	77	151	9497	98674	209447
9:	22	238	3380	50431	609066
10:	16	765	4641	10470	977292
11:	34	866	0607	19441	226400
12:	46	328	8995	32799	297281
13:	20	462	8549	95974	380737
14:	22	775	4403	31419	513111
15:	24	385	7496	60847	280369
16:	62	089	7790	88012	174350
17:	92	474	1172	60094	911477
18:	90	144	7615	48863	365051
19:	87	592	2665	22201	630423
20:	79	832	7150	15734	243302
21:	74	267	8236	80420	545094
22:	16	439	0940	73451	686247
23:	21	127	0080	16180	107190
24:	57	926	8079	28034	302293
25:	91	021	7521	13038	599034
26:	17	517	8668	55385	498003
27:	86	395	3443	42278	620398
28:	36	610	0262	81606	806708
29:	75	784	7596	32489	364373
30:	04	314	7991	21136	006189

DECEMBER	2-DIGIT	3-DIGIT	4-DIGIT	5-DIGIT	6-DIGIT
1:	88	033	5469	14859	914596
2:	32	966	2138	06767	136049
3:	83	942	2295	02563	457887
4:	38	046	5287	13920	556348
5:	55	258	1391	66801	467888
6:	80	907	7922	65487	617853
7:	65	765	8719	34181	673672
8:	82	844	5890	33362	058273
9:	48	735	9785	44599	667409
10:	55	925	0319	15301	472311
11:	36	942	6636	10467	654857
12:	17	109	0381	15044	903951
13:	26	728	1655	07583	994910
14:	92	096	8161	01747	016867
15:	99	119	2445	60530	422744
16:	16	454	3518	58459	897644
17:	39	684	7740	44091	905773
18:	22	466	8963	88821	542597
19:	68	232	1228	10841	077734
20:	60	361	6629	60464	922712
21:	43	714	8518	50369	145421
22:	74	057	1033	37880	314212
23:	53	085	8857	06327	588395
24:	26	496	4998	46919	836151
25:	01	211	5256	88385	221972
26:	75	075	3468	97101	780990
27:	51	457	0939	86186	002396
28:	10	395	0481	98860	363120
29:	65	546	6849	49113	722644
30:	71	487	2991	33116	049437
31:	66	098	3876	25526	551975

JANUARY	2-DIGIT	3-DIGIT	4-DIGIT	5-DIGIT	6-DIGIT
1:	88	427	6875	18122	086455
2:	89	474	9327	07516	198768
3:	85	205	6071	87252	028796
4:	91	513	5299	24707	370679
5:	49	758	9635	43842	531917
6:	01	495	2702	27969	934055
7:	02	887	6711	02940	933412
8:	39	510	8863	55324	748310
9:	47	065	2057	21887	513073
10:	20	076	6128	46920	819889
11:	64	241	9321	38449	137913
12:	96	996	5676	88445	945341
13:	30	798	2772	19500	696245
14:	90	475	8173	07269	147347
15:	82	886	1090	20251	742703
16:	44	662	8123	42021	634197
17:	56	274	3311	32928	721385
18:	17	608	7144	70376	286606
19:	56	837	5783	03820	716346
20:	82	070	9378	20819	566405
21:	87	572	3888	34687	991143
22:	60	575	0030	05510	581479
23:	06	767	0061	89260	211981
24:	63	648	3405	26969	678060
25:	76	275	5507	94655	092737
26:	44	451	5663	58208	243940
27:	23	532	0325	37319	145441
28:	91	116	2853	59964	773421
29:	69	620	8907	22262	692488
30:	88	283	2615	81919	670534
31:	12	964	9547	53375	722596

FEBRUARY	2-DIGIT	3-DIGIT	4-DIGIT	5-DIGIT	6-DIGIT
1:	23	094	7539	56390	086496
2:	76	190	4183	81922	680596
3:	58	494	7803	01431	725138
4:	45	287	9214	35248	742072
5:	52	317	3010	06079	971078
6:	40	480	7922	75648	059492
7:	66	708	4102	52625	511821
8:	23	012	8311	05136	994285
9:	14	863	9861	45975	833034
10:	90	094	3004	60721	908913
11:	23	050	6523	99047	230744
12:	21	338	2540	99994	391979
13:	90	562	1065	23643	878238
14:	17	513	1812	23451	112220
15:	05	839	6599	36942	521860
16:	69	076	0205	70631	410801
17:	11	218	4604	62917	969786
18:	98	509	6466	00245	315469
19:	65	261	3487	38827	893287
20:	03	536	1461	86317	289093
21:	75	610	3976	84995	366285
22:	09	406	1987	61593	454757
23:	56	790	9245	74581	826776
24:	37	583	1975	92490	344300
25:	85	699	6636	40078	983567
26:	32	817	9956	49176	228876
27:	35	772	4616	43087	988646
28:	23	368	0318	42899	972965
29:	45	105	6611	44091	027504

MARCH	2-DIGIT	3-DIGIT	4-DIGIT	5-DIGIT	6-DIGIT
1:	27	280	8681	83996	824241
2:	96	173	0896	16053	275306
3:	26	084	4716	45346	973591
4:	22	233	4911	99863	211336
5:	68	462	3286	49114	035017
6:	41	715	6015	78910	474813
7:	88	261	2107	63795	848126
8:	95	538	8725	17685	131022
9:	08	437	7263	54133	259668
10:	24	538	5864	20943	509957
11:	10	959	3875	08708	506831
12:	11	111	2376	40394	693137
13:	67	877	6222	20253	334923
14:	21	966	2301	44283	211363
15:	42	442	3136	81606	536922
16:	16	238	3644	34624	215125
17:	48	745	4453	97673	493023
18:	03	822	0080	48424	277825
19:	23	949	7464	60279	499253
20:	41	755	0042	43275	882594
21:	53	661	9146	91772	728900
22:	51	590	1586	40768	698173
23:	39	008	0501	19878	033778
24:	15	789	0933	48800	171192
25:	04	535	4064	58024	116591
26:	54	725	8938	36629	118463
27:	14	699	0350	43467	648613
28:	66	440	4359	88827	319260
29:	87	248	6925	07079	809232
30:	86	865	6103	27592	474792
31:	29	498	9070	11472	825509

APRIL	2-DIGIT	3-DIGIT	4-DIGIT	5-DIGIT	6-DIGIT
1:	53	839	1335	90082	281609
2:	98	015	2872	18121	477972
3:	86	095	9215	65865	537544
4:	20	852	8456	29918	377610
5:	82	329	0632	32867	241478
6:	37	930	8656	58397	539467
7:	97	977	5187	82049	242693
8:	41	685	7213	86253	799123
9:	48	506	8286	24960	616604
10:	41	215	3336	52876	869416
11:	06	013	8637	16051	518768
12:	01	129	5532	45219	141708
13:	91	391	2602	27722	777165
14:	99	674	1730	35938	647319
15:	92	659	0632	72638	011827
16:	54	581	4679	00426	702542
17:	47	189	0569	89326	172440
18:	28	191	9447	39329	920847
19:	29	555	5136	53941	763436
20:	71	305	4603	32300	174314
21:	30	869	2075	76406	908937
22:	24	517	1831	81608	711301
23:	22	314	5852	80545	366915
24:	01	750	6046	08082	117877
25:	82	584	4635	31862	383199
26:	98	483	5018	10341	119084
27:	18	418	4107	38761	811097
28:	00	024	9484	24020	962246
29:	32	250	5500	17053	965406
30:	61	893	3825	49362	218231

MAY	2-DIGIT	3-DIGIT	4-DIGIT	5-DIGIT	6-DIGIT
1:	11	479	5363	83052	551337
2:	26	404	4691	79976	707531
3:	17	386	4233	23829	910180
4:	33	851	0400	72196	036271
5:	80	482	7157	50932	958358
6:	91	860	4252	28030	535693
7:	20	641	0080	75402	870078
8:	88	449	8305	85751	057612
9:	08	003	2388	05139	586505
10:	80	272	4038	48237	410200
11:	66	262	2828	09399	829919
12:	21	680	3023	52748	159263
13:	13	247	1210	83300	168655
14:	21	420	1768	51247	589658
15:	52	889	5387	59590	620330
16:	85	913	6611	74708	822976
17:	27	971	9290	73143	033188
18:	00	161	1730	76716	989899
19:	62	136	1461	14922	256509
20:	37	599	8756	18873	715071
21:	84	539	5199	96475	260243
22:	37	324	0061	61661	711327
23:	54	485	3431	82799	305412
24:	33	947	0989	70942	370032
25:	12	868	8299	35747	430935
26:	34	609	1579	29916	933444
27:	27	602	4472	78534	729502
28:	38	251	4579	13978	401448
29:	48	057	5576	39137	572671
30:	98	004	2947	13226	492984
31:	58	810	7496	04257	359406

JUNE	2-DIGIT	3-DIGIT	4-DIGIT	5-DIGIT	6-DIGIT
1:	65	195	5683	61877	961051
2:	56	554	8763	11280	059491
3:	25	004	1830	22386	053882
4:	81	791	5626	22828	611597
5:	84	768	0124	26529	130406
6:	19	934	9265	39010	576470
7:	07	616	5632	32674	909563
8:	43	348	2402	67619	458542
9:	62	561	6925	62663	263433
10:	14	249	1724	86941	381936
11:	71	090	4629	97670	334905
12:	35	716	3807	52439	210093
13:	59	128	4716	58526	710048
14:	83	546	4710	08523	083372
15:	09	152	3901	33300	430310
16:	57	481	3280	74144	749612
17:	19	471	5030	78724	321141
18:	45	848	7583	65113	734548
19:	30	710	9321	84492	058876
20:	77	205	5049	48049	828624
21:	06	196	8079	16867	393892
22:	37	358	7333	04886	784746
23:	42	543	7552	82989	479210
24:	70	422	2025	65735	383226
25:	72	358	3813	53381	620989
26:	93	942	1736	83929	445940
27:	60	403	2885	47352	712611
28:	40	641	6856	47792	112209
29:	75	405	4026	66055	563286
30:	45	751	9365	66236	220144

JULY	2-DIGIT	3-DIGIT	4-DIGIT	5-DIGIT	6-DIGIT
1:	19	592	8782	75709	809186
2:	95	037	5488	73016	513677
3:	39	546	1391	50369	981104
4:	15	511	7081	40015	059494
5:	98	412	5318	82864	075229
6:	66	233	9942	87444	376972
7:	33	064	8543	65421	535663
8:	62	253	6742	71884	346825
9:	38	484	7414	65420	657394
10:	00	223	2678	21821	430884
11:	28	563	5205	84623	493043
12:	20	881	1900	70507	737035
13:	48	483	7514	76214	708815
14:	03	541	7658	88823	716977
15:	74	414	3436	67309	229524
16:	13	366	8223	81420	547567
17:	22	476	3072	33807	356264
18:	39	592	8587	87943	934043
19:	31	855	2922	01813	411429
20:	72	859	6391	68621	174966
21:	81	976	0225	64671	594674
22:	07	960	7847	37132	965443
23:	64	202	5193	63289	678711
24:	27	382	2602	93466	778474
25:	27	000	2734	13732	392613
26:	66	420	9666	20064	457237
27:	17	748	9409	45347	434019
28:	14	036	7006	04132	701902
29:	56	220	7264	02188	008686
30:	11	293	4848	70508	450986
31:	52	862	7627	28412	370040

AUGUST	2-DIGIT	3-DIGIT	4-DIGIT	5-DIGIT	6-DIGIT
1:	79	042	3857	66362	486131
2:	15	264	2721	03565	592152
3:	27	688	1611	61722	312964
4:	71	238	6799	55261	242078
5:	82	886	0432	01369	679334
6:	74	806	9685	18999	398899
7:	94	805	9490	31233	523756
8:	30	622	6925	60030	421508
9:	64	935	1925	78281	615370
10:	30	400	4014	02937	045081
11:	29	949	6542	57204	935295
12:	28	813	1793	33049	237034
13:	22	131	6906	61095	479846
14:	87	878	1843	02942	525633
15:	15	814	4095	47039	325476
16:	22	233	1881	70565	328610
17:	19	706	2627	00621	642939
18:	55	044	7991	32303	914590
19:	17	854	6379	16049	656761
20:	65	174	6347	55639	309824
21:	60	549	9240	45035	448462
22:	40	780	9120	22763	259621
23:	33	604	5249	66367	548842
24:	20	901	7251	47605	662426
25:	99	945	2414	60968	213858
26:	48	839	0576	13977	687496
27:	34	678	5463	86938	911446
28:	32	757	4277	45345	841798
29:	49	627	1774	01870	124736
30:	81	051	7439	42964	193149
31:	12	663	8348	16807	522468

SEPTEMBER	2-DIGIT	3-DIGIT	4-DIGIT	5-DIGIT	6-DIGIT
1:	95	635	6285	87133	687526
2:	92	066	8801	90456	434699
3:	82	722	5168	65676	347484
4:	47	407	2540	85188	280358
5:	32	760	6272	06577	110306
6:	68	043	0331	55699	615352
7:	44	151	4465	11093	043811
8:	46	636	8123	23577	108420
9:	95	227	3914	17495	105280
10:	83	643	6354	07269	417133
11:	41	537	5042	28663	997420
12:	00	336	0607	65484	147363
13:	26	432	8367	92402	180564
14:	96	755	3857	93341	972916
15:	70	659	2508	29037	150510
16:	84	937	3957	13038	016876
17:	98	744	1692	11726	923378
18:	08	558	1673	70000	811081
19:	56	478	2207	62416	524384
20:	91	157	9767	76280	521219
21:	47	403	4628	53254	789106
22:	62	100	8374	11788	117237
23:	91	615	0274	44724	324913
24:	80	585	1473	41520	649223
25:	41	725	6598	02686	417701
26:	98	402	1209	48424	156094
27:	85	979	2583	10342	415195
28:	62	570	2251	34619	046946
29:	43	108	9923	53633	422749
30:	31	565	9277	49177	376931

OCTOBER	2-DIGIT	3-DIGIT	4-DIGIT	5-DIGIT	6-DIGIT
1:	34	174	0789	10219	037539
2:	21	092	3305	54320	127292
3:	81	225	0500	71823	284759
4:	29	033	1950	99235	230162
5:	62	631	0312	38319	253382
6:	97	047	4986	20320	443437
7:	97	084	7414	04572	519342
8:	62	211	7458	55698	885138
9:	93	696	8417	19505	298528
10:	02	309	1661	47040	621586
11:	65	491	8970	76969	669928
12:	51	790	3066	19686	103442
13:	54	359	1768	53880	326115
14:	13	308	5187	68250	492365
15:	37	604	7226	69442	112800
16:	32	737	5500	57831	202518
17:	30	370	4654	91646	462913
18:	12	551	9264	62350	860036
19:	69	872	0814	59778	619748
20:	26	206	4384	23580	684379
21:	34	561	3211	59273	598388
22:	80	732	7332	47290	397021
23:	19	614	2320	33678	514318
24:	71	219	6968	67747	602798
25:	64	630	3311	91144	017512
26:	05	306	2565	38385	065785
27:	40	014	1956	74204	515567
28:	85	770	2351	49052	407055
29:	50	461	9509	19002	557016
30:	62	912	6818	27218	591487
31:	04	443	9672	61783	210714

NOVEMBER	2-DIGIT	3-DIGIT	4-DIGIT	5-DIGIT	6-DIGIT
1:	91	201	4176	83243	291031
2:	54	577	6768	79039	316759
3:	66	634	2671	83991	179371
4:	51	657	9390	17807	630409
5:	76	990	2144	84369	263380
6:	66	500	3079	11409	483595
7:	22	149	0425	96788	959751
8:	25	853	8060	84682	814832
9:	42	453	3060	86501	416441
10:	44	523	5363	85685	393263
11:	86	718	4490	88636	579566
12:	59	076	4848	18563	200004
13:	38	617	7665	67431	311069
14:	10	692	0080	65861	321371
15:	41	169	2056	75458	139220
16:	41	914	2138	05761	669287
17:	29	117	7489	02309	481748
18:	94	240	6592	02751	473567
19:	06	414	8995	12729	501809
20:	52	928	4158	72135	974205
21:	81	031	1692	84747	331126
22:	43	163	1887	55075	252723
23:	88	124	9860	00552	820473
24:	65	652	3819	19816	839919
25:	32	732	3387	84613	657360
26:	80	427	5852	68372	991752
27:	04	157	1053	99677	221981
28:	74	700	3769	48297	281625
29:	43	561	0149	79728	915833
30:	26	188	4948	06637	981731

DECEMBER	2-DIGIT	3-DIGIT	4-DIGIT	5-DIGIT	6-DIGIT
1:	05	831	6692	54323	867568
2:	79	104	4804	22014	927115
3:	81	691	6466	73266	723216
4:	11	866	3700	13356	334929
5:	36	183	8060	35000	690651
6:	48	104	8029	39077	684985
7:	94	735	9691	92962	323010
8:	74	223	6724	41712	701289
9:	39	125	1698	47543	346836
10:	68	813	8932	46855	615968
11:	34	653	3518	26216	727008
12:	63	557	8355	11847	708813
13:	62	732	5387	58583	259037
14:	32	193	1805	85000	846837
15:	84	165	9541	61974	844938
16:	50	316	9334	12097	918352
17:	34	158	7696	21570	612862
18:	53	865	2784	69439	372524
19:	45	858	2251	18187	560162
20:	78	713	0137	28161	864391
21:	64	211	6931	97860	778489
22:	30	737	7740	45098	372535
23:	75	186	3769	89075	518736
24:	12	038	0978	22010	160515
25:	10	205	9026	25084	994259
26:	71	693	2282	33174	894538
27:	58	897	8060	97861	656758
28:	92	767	2860	95161	288476
29:	85	107	4923	80419	683087
30:	91	484	1755	83871	854364
31:	89	285	7772	33493	778487

JANUARY	2-DIGIT	3-DIGIT	4-DIGIT	5-DIGIT	6-DIGIT
1:	77	099	3217	06644	488607
2:	93	708	8342	13853	178047
3:	30	594	3380	08647	905192
4:	94	463	9007	67932	756471
5:	18	938	7835	89826	025621
6:	59	028	1969	61031	137931
7:	82	245	4170	80289	946611
8:	13	112	0136	53127	523120
9:	23	061	7107	22824	279101
10:	21	479	1642	84623	805415
11:	91	003	3869	16301	162411
12:	70	752	5745	14483	004966
13:	23	410	9603	59085	434653
14:	90	788	4553	00553	386370
15:	57	455	4860	13538	435953
16:	21	489	6310	37698	631028
17:	39	006	4685	49412	967924
18:	57	758	7628	64295	849363
19:	47	056	0319	87316	518764
20:	17	722	2044	95288	120360
21:	16	949	8286	63106	117259
22:	50	378	3311	86499	252062
23:	38	341	3154	39764	241473
24:	22	713	2897	67680	954711
25:	80	314	0294	35125	094630
26:	63	188	0111	17368	691238
27:	33	028	6015	80922	408337
28:	94	912	1718	53756	800404
29:	61	149	8224	29475	402053
30:	08	231	3111	72825	297294
31:	91	495	2339	07647	797252

FEBRUARY	2-DIGIT	3-DIGIT	4-DIGIT	5-DIGIT	6-DIGIT
1:	12	959	2690	31988	336813
2:	67	295	3261	42965	637314
3:	67	391	5564	60593	034444
4:	80	632	4089	78978	731383
5:	86	956	5237	72012	326736
6:	91	902	8794	96036	156755
7:	35	711	9980	49802	601567
8:	26	329	7477	01683	109056
9:	02	789	3732	44155	247687
10:	26	994	6636	11473	121619
11:	70	934	5187	15299	880090
12:	59	533	1404	08205	077691
13:	41	940	0557	66366	982945
14:	27	098	5155	53882	066391
15:	00	188	9491	07893	240190
16:	78	366	1743	32926	711323
17:	81	077	8888	32867	389534
18:	59	506	7728	06326	604657
19:	63	572	0934	96855	920210
20:	91	290	4102	97042	057620
21:	96	733	2690	45787	087141
22:	71	376	3248	59777	323638
23:	93	055	7295	27723	343062
24:	91	477	2771	29661	243354
25:	80	417	4610	25713	985496
26:	23	159	3512	92025	678715
27:	00	790	7144	53944	799822
28:	02	442	5996	78348	157987
29:	15	716	7031	69503	862493

MARCH	2-DIGIT	3-DIGIT	4-DIGIT	5-DIGIT	6-DIGIT
1:	37	782	7044	19441	538773
2:	27	449	2019	89140	722657
3:	42	626	6780	34242	571420
4:	32	749	6347	01682	230787
5:	40	759	8612	94091	331745
6:	05	178	4428	20130	957268
7:	91	488	3355	53438	186242
8:	80	558	3713	10343	398932
9:	24	600	6316	84682	962887
10:	54	029	1077	34430	587100
11:	10	012	0055	00491	070780
12:	36	322	1379	99425	838063
13:	06	303	9252	39390	670540
14:	68	885	7577	74332	765292
15:	97	839	8738	77533	161133
16:	31	517	0350	59899	135397
17:	31	835	4145	03752	772149
18:	54	602	9271	58396	407674
19:	13	476	2050	84057	156092
20:	54	275	0312	80103	957255
21:	19	349	0620	52311	664258
22:	14	907	1241	23640	720120
23:	59	406	4484	27466	044488
24:	41	913	2796	24642	732655
25:	11	973	4873	35878	611577
26:	67	709	9359	04446	671196
27:	03	400	9215	23074	366908
28:	45	829	8016	97673	075181
29:	33	701	7056	92083	852450
30:	00	785	9233	22010	308570
31:	21	781	8098	73012	164918

APRIL	2-DIGIT	3-DIGIT	4-DIGIT	5-DIGIT	6-DIGIT
1:	11	669	2734	27531	142940
2:	70	501	9654	47422	143560
3:	33	412	2195	12477	848105
4:	36	775	5689	65362	213873
5:	51	681	5582	55890	667418
6:	43	550	9566	55949	972946
7:	27	046	5846	22007	568295
8:	33	902	4848	33369	417094
9:	96	524	2458	84496	973532
10:	59	267	1561	33613	728239
11:	01	858	4190	01308	511800
12:	64	355	4221	52814	971667
13:	56	108	8180	47731	240785
14:	09	106	6705	95727	371903
15:	40	138	7439	12346	397677
16:	44	129	3957	92968	115935
17:	19	210	7301	77340	516846
18:	66	814	0017	23327	734564
19:	74	256	7653	56644	602207
20:	17	298	1837	88821	272811
21:	20	686	7276	12975	823017
22:	04	687	3091	37002	409547
23:	73	450	3462	90895	686242
24:	06	910	4321	25463	627902
25:	40	158	2131	81110	154232
26:	13	524	0419	44153	491149
27:	01	144	7452	11346	289736
28:	39	092	1824	32611	551388
29:	01	745	8794	05577	689993
30:	82	885	5175	49548	519960

MAY	2-DIGIT	3-DIGIT	4-DIGIT	5-DIGIT	6-DIGIT
1:	44	817	2834	40958	036287
2:	24	028	4434	12537	301688
3:	31	952	9986	79349	874412
4:	34	026	9277	71511	193734
5:	55	778	4064	28413	787881
6:	39	016	9353	02498	793538
7:	05	760	7389	97417	654877
8:	34	062	1146	37128	363161
9:	41	262	1705	23519	099003
10:	54	883	4722	47294	851249
11:	10	872	6736	36067	923368
12:	78	229	0155	99112	852506
13:	32	048	1366	58020	228260
14:	45	269	6617	38510	305448
15:	06	447	0086	54630	372573
16:	78	495	4082	03002	979216
17:	11	886	8392	71572	091483
18:	05	683	5576	86185	960396
19:	31	039	8180	62537	457874
20:	66	013	1498	02246	139834
21:	89	607	8920	90645	894545
22:	15	712	5036	08271	593984
23:	42	650	9384	24393	819226
24:	82	805	0708	68750	599070
25:	89	122	7765	39073	500543
26:	41	022	0281	98986	168678
27:	12	887	7075	33809	964747
28:	53	971	8700	40141	595267
29:	96	102	1592	59147	062615
30:	81	042	2113	71007	304167
31:	93	804	0149	50115	487124

JUNE	2-DIGIT	3-DIGIT	4-DIGIT	5-DIGIT	6-DIGIT
1:	57	553	1924	01621	898935
2:	82	656	9195	30041	755266
3:	12	807	9579	13165	161131
4:	99	813	8079	40207	677457
5:	88	614	2514	21444	389462
6:	25	402	0589	38950	705046
7:	41	317	8311	62346	823649
8:	38	841	9421	13730	636075
9:	41	465	0482	30483	625353
10:	86	906	7101	62660	105316
11:	56	142	4396	90957	314204
12:	97	164	1881	85370	545700
13:	77	613	8475	07140	305402
14:	04	619	9471	00054	411458
15:	88	437	7458	41899	134810
16:	88	720	8430	92146	612205
17:	86	646	9930	90457	312968
18:	44	646	0287	15739	263426
19:	68	328	3694	65985	444709
20:	22	102	7050	68438	804156
21:	37	124	8023	64108	294111
22:	61	491	8707	92777	063869
23:	20	810	2200	43030	587711
24:	85	403	2294	24897	274690
25:	36	582	6718	40770	290393
26:	05	311	4678	11593	610944
27:	91	957	0757	97478	986729
28:	03	164	0563	11725	045109
29:	45	633	7609	30483	895139
30:	45	557	1053	71072	360033

JULY	2-DIGIT	3-DIGIT	4-DIGIT	5-DIGIT	6-DIGIT
1:	92	965	4999	92962	757114
2:	81	420	4628	37442	210724
3:	51	472	8775	94468	373167
4:	09	340	0099	65803	639795
5:	70	052	6943	61598	099626
6:	90	306	1806	72827	471673
7:	87	677	4547	53568	054510
8:	42	432	8468	28532	711309
9:	68	235	3882	90954	304142
10:	50	634	3625	37315	648627
11:	79	282	9365	20193	299182
12:	95	121	1027	76090	765263
13:	81	155	7671	04254	201288
14:	24	773	1090	32424	117866
15:	52	255	3117	50427	424624
16:	74	053	4177	16493	928428
17:	83	425	0958	00991	489857
18:	59	068	5996	25397	545713
19:	48	646	1209	18813	827384
20:	70	164	2998	76211	090270
21:	53	632	9290	99115	053210
22:	12	730	6711	01934	466650
23:	86	684	4057	55069	772170
24:	13	260	2307	10718	430293
25:	70	232	3731	82300	748342
26:	35	157	6611	45097	494266
27:	12	262	8650	39011	602794
28:	91	117	8769	30666	996164
29:	30	864	8248	73769	300411
30:	91	718	4591	35312	110310
31:	41	557	3819	16177	636700

AUGUST	2-DIGIT	3-DIGIT	4-DIGIT	5-DIGIT	6-DIGIT
1:	06	576	2882	05824	577097
2:	26	447	6203	18685	551336
3:	84	700	3474	49737	249591
4:	75	165	2602	51521	527492
5:	03	755	1718	52750	333643
6:	08	323	3418	39768	425914
7:	75	425	3361	61657	109044
8:	31	651	9942	43028	831173
9:	60	448	3110	24770	442807
10:	05	740	3355	58082	856222
11:	46	523	3123	08965	223246
12:	42	902	5375	91207	523743
13:	69	484	3135	48357	899525
14:	97	284	9453	02125	936558
15:	55	206	2182	56267	021212
16:	16	834	8261	47417	080849
17:	29	774	7665	68437	777832
18:	64	518	4886	66116	312979
19:	74	975	1805	86627	222001
20:	91	759	4534	70380	740834
21:	58	095	0199	95661	125395
22:	89	974	2565	52185	816113
23:	45	095	1943	91016	201890
24:	11	539	4083	05634	821141
25:	61	305	8192	80232	963518
26:	46	373	5136	80919	250220
27:	36	806	4390	57772	732673
28:	87	223	4421	27722	612848
29:	50	023	7778	38073	392602
30:	36	986	7094	49176	498662
31:	94	317	8568	51499	137894

SEPTEMBER	2-DIGIT	3-DIGIT	4-DIGIT	5-DIGIT	6-DIGIT
1:	98	607	9942	40395	989247
2:	00	134	3311	16110	570772
3:	64	050	2740	73896	566397
4:	31	757	5858	13730	948447
5:	11	587	2451	76277	050729
6:	08	174	5331	00928	295998
7:	65	011	7395	61220	031880
8:	13	538	2997	29162	702545
9:	20	702	5112	49805	193788
10:	03	632	2709	03945	686222
11:	78	957	3556	03380	168693
12:	25	624	3136	65174	944669
13:	61	737	3857	09152	656767
14:	80	392	2106	35810	789112
15:	77	317	4133	91959	596525
16:	08	277	6222	91648	367507
17:	59	082	7521	10406	757109
18:	67	203	8869	57272	731436
19:	34	705	3882	47544	225105
20:	30	843	2997	96918	531910
21:	44	574	4672	17560	891360
22:	53	004	9133	73708	402662
23:	41	812	4133	66993	937796
24:	49	533	4992	56138	866895
25:	58	339	3618	70880	324229
26:	40	386	8769	19499	087762
27:	76	096	8060	55071	486122
28:	17	639	2420	62916	091517
29:	36	479	2402	50181	399527
30:	55	340	2333	47484	623467

OCTOBER	2-DIGIT	3-DIGIT	4-DIGIT	5-DIGIT	6-DIGIT
1:	22	038	7257	23581	414593
2:	75	910	92159	61408	343670
3:	24	058	3794	23828	883856
4:	49	350	7263	74204	055139
5:	03	072	0256	44782	916489
6:	51	703	6586	65927	583347
7:	92	333	7985	46166	615314
8:	40	842	4152	97165	583331
9:	48	787	0708	84561	177453
10:	00	749	7364	56393	244613
11:	34	297	0456	77906	748327
12:	33	420	0550	13731	514344
13:	03	390	4547	70000	541295
14:	07	827	8255	54003	269667
15:	35	589	6228	42271	008053
16:	77	245	9572	93779	329927
17:	94	953	1661	88814	430928
18:	78	793	3549	08960	890749
19:	78	613	6893	49301	198752
20:	41	659	8794	25647	485465
21:	50	420	9566	73387	926492
22:	35	267	0438	47733	102792
23:	34	061	5889	85307	203786
24:	72	980	0802	95034	726380
25:	13	917	6567	95596	609102
26:	78	265	2683	94158	979832
27:	00	494	7445	76149	774680
28:	22	605	5808	74455	560789
29:	97	544	9643	14172	506162
30:	15	563	8004	79978	569538
31:	42	341	3418	23956	742063

NOVEMBER	2-DIGIT	3-DIGIT	4-DIGIT	5-DIGIT	6-DIGIT
1:	04	245	3449	34685	859350
2:	87	969	6893	07517	494879
3:	18	355	4215	93657	264644
4:	34	597	5739	54319	831182
5:	48	073	3412	75966	943442
6:	96	949	2565	80169	769659
7:	63	316	7590	16742	736388
8:	11	698	6178	68120	607834
9:	37	655	6535	90770	716365
10:	99	023	1197	42902	025614
11:	13	212	3939	40075	095236
12:	23	362	7646	51057	415861
13:	16	520	5407	64796	712606
14:	25	423	1097	67621	632922
15:	68	743	9133	08584	415223
16:	67	254	3317	07897	006790
17:	50	747	9183	81109	440279
18:	10	250	0306	02501	829924
19:	36	792	8782	43465	638550
20:	19	909	6103	40771	316717
21:	89	917	8870	20132	697544
22:	78	367	7659	03628	934066
23:	32	216	8229	73828	891987
24:	62	835	9704	49172	044434
25:	93	059	5206	49110	834314
26:	61	032	0670	34996	236423
27:	58	846	3612	36688	275935
28:	77	725	7559	61597	073302
29:	06	700	8669	74835	385073
30:	99	161	7646	47418	107174

DECEMBER	2-DIGIT	3-DIGIT	4-DIGIT	5-DIGIT	6-DIGIT
1:	89	641	0275	63168	745221
2:	52	632	0871	56954	159860
3:	74	690	8443	76341	392643
4:	13	702	1949	23581	980490
5:	67	713	0299	65678	939705
6:	23	816	7772	76903	857524
7:	18	929	6097	65802	031312
8:	56	673	6831	09400	438402
9:	35	059	3135	04946	820488
10:	67	494	8825	51182	819841
11:	30	604	7489	43087	718859
12:	64	717	6366	45034	718249
13:	89	432	3072	20628	514338
14:	89	278	8788	89830	062008
15:	90	164	3362	07079	121605
16:	67	092	9126	83933	900168
17:	61	767	7301	49741	016191
18:	47	651	0043	89704	361917
19:	43	929	3135	22384	774034
20:	85	715	3417	76907	354338
21:	31	763	9585	05573	505551
22:	40	173	4710	55572	365628
23:	42	082	9133	82611	289732
24:	66	685	8336	72133	530039
25:	26	304	5532	30414	924618
26:	33	484	6755	10656	114702
27:	50	205	0250	68186	150452
28:	21	971	9553	46789	533778
29:	31	141	2596	63920	400162
30:	20	198	9879	43904	307934
31:	14	325	8280	46353	022511

JANUARY	2-DIGIT	3-DIGIT	4-DIGIT	5-DIGIT	6-DIGIT
1:	36	586	3574	72704	676176
2:	86	972	2577	16929	709481
3:	68	385	0814	19000	277168
4:	56	730	4610	81297	439697
5:	51	543	9133	51374	585859
6:	43	382	2702	40142	309219
7:	99	481	1705	11346	829308
8:	46	289	9729	38889	955353
9:	02	987	5871	52502	716325
10:	23	307	6341	68497	649256
11:	30	817	2207	36443	398893
12:	79	588	3731	40516	044468
13:	13	854	2032	13106	273445
14:	85	439	4823	19943	402015
15:	04	922	1743	58898	836814
16:	82	647	3869	58085	866284
17:	93	054	1379	57020	225787
18:	40	233	3430	88701	635432
19:	77	982	2634	82867	545720
20:	94	567	9239	29223	870080
21:	29	153	9522	15990	621020
22:	40	329	5074	87447	969193
23:	09	368	3776	67683	112829
24:	48	421	6567	31109	162362
25:	37	114	3914	29668	480444
26:	91	131	1348	15675	207560
27:	49	422	5908	12228	204463
28:	56	258	5475	96099	350614
29:	29	663	7527	13980	009931
30:	62	436	5688	91335	233895
31:	63	251	1617	81107	144169

FEBRUARY	2-DIGIT	3-DIGIT	4-DIGIT	5-DIGIT	6-DIGIT
1:	35	594	2426	55324	435937
2:	76	944	9033	65546	193166
3:	98	913	7897	08651	523738
4:	54	373	7376	68186	420237
5:	80	622	3505	55201	788495
6:	87	814	6134	87382	913327
7:	91	461	5990	03379	872582
8:	82	472	4992	58770	708821
9:	18	653	3418	79540	196264
10:	91	077	9384	14233	377586
11:	81	863	5325	50305	760921
12:	47	848	5344	77846	564531
13:	86	894	0205	97609	003053
14:	76	614	4390	77842	528144
15:	65	757	8813	51561	019380
16:	92	872	9434	84745	574588
17:	18	208	2702	54948	420839
18:	57	282	6498	28412	491771
19:	06	758	1209	06640	452220
20:	72	676	6949	67805	194374
21:	35	747	8424	15551	951635
22:	56	913	2897	71319	263400
23:	94	454	4898	33492	942804
24:	47	684	0476	12724	169313
25:	88	639	5676	30229	649214
26:	53	100	7351	62038	917066
27:	06	298	2000	26337	348126
28:	69	186	8117	02565	902052
29:	92	879	1448	57706	068324

MARCH	2-DIGIT	3-DIGIT	4-DIGIT	5-DIGIT	6-DIGIT
1:	48	287	6975	47981	572055
2:	08	501	3894	08650	915254
3:	40	994	7263	15988	759013
4:	15	375	5890	87320	137310
5:	78	526	0413	84995	784126
6:	79	528	5011	17934	774664
7:	78	059	8531	12850	017458
8:	57	451	3920	62853	167444
9:	01	073	7753	83869	140412
10:	75	907	6605	81294	117263
11:	34	785	7853	46977	263410
12:	23	782	6416	04380	006848
13:	71	009	1316	17119	465437
14:	34	633	8826	57453	970454
15:	94	056	1893	50115	439068
16:	90	903	6291	35124	380678
17:	59	809	9999	65170	030014
18:	68	676	7345	13041	757152
19:	85	729	5996	51369	671203
20:	49	321	7245	44031	409604
21:	04	713	5595	26905	605931
22:	19	293	2841	80414	768432
23:	98	423	5243	87759	954749
24:	83	623	0607	49052	555110
25:	72	036	8581	66931	727675
26:	28	401	1511	42024	374474
27:	54	153	6561	72572	363741
28:	69	265	1661	44407	885129
29:	05	072	9171	68309	797893
30:	10	100	2451	35499	813618
31:	39	592	4503	58645	156785

APRIL	2-DIGIT	3-DIGIT	4-DIGIT	5-DIGIT	6-DIGIT
1:	82	993	2263	42773	019351
2:	76	188	8368	22013	614743
3:	11	569	3443	27472	403309
4:	78	703	5469	75087	038777
5:	15	314	6115	54191	867506
6:	32	730	6912	95286	528139
7:	51	646	3054	60844	540093
8:	75	210	3486	37821	426525
9:	50	711	6655	86063	312954
10:	42	804	4227	84373	283504
11:	59	756	9591	07521	383210
12:	27	812	6536	91776	183128
13:	53	849	4948	32610	107222
14:	46	018	2633	51244	283486
15:	73	206	0043	15676	381940
16:	44	498	8116	58149	356253
17:	09	157	7069	17055	975468
18:	07	424	2081	97418	220773
19:	26	865	3242	41397	853726
20:	40	020	5683	76594	072672
21:	13	356	3555	28346	827422
22:	74	473	3311	90138	550750
23:	52	480	7759	38131	089646
24:	07	208	3261	73582	432786
25:	35	925	9955	84432	440976
26:	22	482	6799	25650	913368
27:	67	178	0846	77784	248941
28:	65	762	6724	72949	405164
29:	62	427	7333	90081	567657
30:	84	636	2759	65923	816747

MAY	2-DIGIT	3-DIGIT	4-DIGIT	5-DIGIT	6-DIGIT
1:	68	967	7860	25585	857503
2:	59	166	3060	13480	008695
3:	99	918	5149	11157	951621
4:	43	072	6837	39953	283477
5:	85	582	0796	64481	986773
6:	53	394	8907	36061	442816
7:	93	365	2602	09278	356857
8:	38	627	2333	20505	136683
9:	59	695	9842	98984	142354
10:	38	281	3939	25269	983615
11:	65	455	2853	33991	753399
12:	67	050	3926	97045	215738
13:	65	840	8963	41771	154872
14:	46	302	7050	71077	112843
15:	51	263	2627	62475	142284
16:	46	986	8016	88132	541944
17:	75	421	1862	92337	934057
18:	44	591	8982	33179	301352
19:	81	731	0494	27632	130997
20:	76	266	0739	41333	215702
21:	92	235	0921	58083	152332
22:	79	675	0212	04822	564563
23:	75	986	5814	20819	984246
24:	58	799	6912	80480	311050
25:	82	738	8261	43778	772162
26:	26	635	3060	70069	929677
27:	79	022	4522	60213	834905
28:	19	364	2144	37319	981124
29:	43	465	8901	62098	518704
30:	23	946	5369	98800	179323
31:	18	125	6504	32992	211354

JUNE	2-DIGIT	3-DIGIT	4-DIGIT	5-DIGIT	6-DIGIT
1:	85	883	0281	92715	123534
2:	48	329	2671	26781	350007
3:	27	785	8775	50052	827368
4:	25	619	4666	14606	546940
5:	02	539	3556	47796	724492
6:	98	240	7514	05825	037525
7:	18	250	7244	22954	147370
8:	83	353	6398	01812	223260
9:	45	638	1435	22573	503665
10:	67	356	8292	17368	961024
11:	82	574	9967	78787	663054
12:	50	481	5256	77219	313570
13:	31	412	3280	88950	861232
14:	76	378	9823	95790	983603
15:	94	422	9064	32864	231416
16:	01	399	1454	10342	536926
17:	99	646	7131	84555	131004
18:	22	187	7715	62289	258398
19:	52	224	7445	87316	683082
20:	77	267	5996	93153	375077
21:	72	623	1824	86568	630425
22:	20	536	9421	45973	806710
23:	06	487	9867	62728	927782
24:	35	640	9622	03444	388876
25:	92	287	4873	27344	545192
26:	73	360	8970	94407	623474
27:	70	011	7659	45412	637939
28:	55	518	3863	16365	112807
29:	89	658	3531	78787	245213
30:	79	359	2232	31425	993663

JULY	2-DIGIT	3-DIGIT	4-DIGIT	5-DIGIT	6-DIGIT
1:	43	512	1354	62039	631018
2:	09	677	3167	78536	009350
3:	34	433	6787	59899	553238
4:	01	062	7169	60093	197525
5:	76	765	7502	96664	703826
6:	33	344	3995	54320	979237
7:	70	649	2483	23894	114101
8:	63	439	7257	84429	552645
9:	13	921	3424	27531	994885
10:	49	925	0582	88947	972901
11:	67	922	7502	97671	170588
12:	86	170	8800	54574	955376
13:	03	454	1178	35063	196882
14:	12	283	9654	49048	518724
15:	41	005	7188	20883	638532
16:	43	659	6554	48927	315448
17:	06	604	0450	86505	870669
18:	45	781	9779	88074	802312
19:	93	728	7677	20002	829274
20:	16	494	2903	85440	516221
21:	78	581	1718	67555	550732
22:	66	230	8211	42687	088377
23:	24	895	4842	39955	605912
24:	02	339	1021	68878	309222
25:	83	888	6247	71824	745187
26:	21	731	4045	03505	720728
27:	51	284	3235	91394	121581
28:	66	626	3819	01371	419611
29:	61	685	2934	69190	146723
30:	46	462	5062	94718	122278
31:	78	857	0312	24529	503054

AUGUST	2-DIGIT	3-DIGIT	4-DIGIT	5-DIGIT	6-DIGIT
1:	63	608	2966	99989	059482
2:	37	379	2584	81738	553247
3:	89	687	7472	00741	698160
4:	68	870	6712	18752	617263
5:	49	137	8461	62097	492380
6:	39	445	2232	00807	198191
7:	41	609	0658	26842	264017
8:	15	660	5168	68308	083941
9:	07	826	2339	83301	152393
10:	84	345	6887	01311	400131
11:	73	810	7596	50933	890151
12:	64	360	7389	36569	516825
13:	07	051	6981	71005	711946
14:	17	501	5971	58400	009958
15:	36	311	5538	23827	735800
16:	27	774	8192	26275	884481
17:	26	477	5563	29976	133503
18:	12	098	9697	55138	324851
19:	44	106	3581	14793	250247
20:	10	680	4240	90264	234577
21:	61	746	2050	72890	247691
22:	99	507	0124	71952	142967
23:	44	376	8559	79915	645465
24:	08	935	8769	57644	482948
25:	85	259	8035	99241	858770
26:	59	966	6937	86629	814221
27:	67	062	9766	72642	318000
28:	33	264	0024	54886	940932
29:	77	604	9064	05886	639163
30:	36	004	0613	84870	978568
31:	32	292	4785	33239	532562

SEPTEMBER	2-DIGIT	3-DIGIT	4-DIGIT	5-DIGIT	6-DIGIT
1:	52	711	4415	98796	142937
2:	97	988	5111	86944	122212
3:	59	970	7878	47861	082730
4:	87	479	8324	15923	703147
5:	07	363	8104	23015	791595
6:	11	682	8838	23203	225116
7:	60	172	4515	67806	490484
8:	78	899	5513	11408	187474
9:	89	998	2282	00931	723902
10:	82	769	7621	55069	354329
11:	43	138	9283	64924	004916
12:	48	068	5500	44031	557659
13:	15	289	4666	74834	776590
14:	96	888	7533	95220	445949
15:	48	133	2131	98548	213246
16:	31	745	6065	69879	025646
17:	02	304	8493	73832	076428
18:	15	548	0168	53695	198766
19:	44	395	4855	67560	465388
20:	59	292	3668	42399	987992
21:	30	557	0952	24396	829289
22:	29	336	8964	16805	496143
23:	87	453	5820	36567	612231
24:	60	520	8725	22949	814873
25:	19	169	6862	60907	898269
26:	17	812	7094	99864	089606
27:	30	482	8405	99177	950958
28:	62	636	8223	70253	639164
29:	78	708	2884	15109	541976
30:	64	513	6416	15547	915249

OCTOBER	2-DIGIT	3-DIGIT	4-DIGIT	5-DIGIT	6-DIGIT
1:	04	206	9189	98482	443429
2:	09	459	7113	53376	018707
3:	81	107	8248	44158	971701
4:	76	903	5005	01181	785386
5:	33	513	0858	70127	642964
6:	87	320	5569	34556	853087
7:	49	051	1322	78909	908917
8:	06	458	0011	59525	252092
9:	96	780	5802	64610	157353
10:	39	964	8430	62535	283494
11:	71	831	9289	56325	882575
12:	36	708	7326	69689	269690
13:	36	056	1536	24832	488611
14:	77	221	2885	74331	199396
15:	05	036	6642	73263	670567
16:	42	759	6372	17371	267197
17:	61	257	5312	22700	901445
18:	90	896	2696	93778	885762
19:	39	225	5501	45038	918952
20:	68	114	9472	75088	752729
21:	29	693	7283	06389	634199
22:	98	977	4528	63167	179324
23:	60	829	8775	63231	669294
24:	86	038	4465	23266	418975
25:	54	229	3116	31983	004316
26:	03	006	4779	01060	312323
27:	49	460	0168	37884	620384
28:	33	768	4202	50240	826786
29:	66	912	3493	63478	408343
30:	09	024	7477	44473	279692
31:	78	811	3117	76400	550116

NOVEMBER	2-DIGIT	3-DIGIT	4-DIGIT	5-DIGIT	6-DIGIT
1:	64	693	3763	54883	470442
2:	49	376	8712	64107	146055
3:	39	915	9635	44848	998679
4:	54	321	7508	28223	910194
5:	36	693	6461	14109	016193
6:	88	355	1259	19943	819857
7:	75	149	4766	15239	156721
8:	04	810	3155	96353	056967
9:	03	922	3324	27283	943463
10:	56	607	5601	21945	792277
11:	21	072	9271	14985	328637
12:	93	580	2477	33113	144844
13:	30	567	5620	77470	654902
14:	77	233	8725	49928	301657
15:	84	565	7703	86378	456628
16:	84	166	9441	51180	793517
17:	46	998	4353	45095	632259
18:	77	307	9465	38884	770911
19:	60	380	5406	58525	561992
20:	61	971	6693	60594	912713
21:	43	663	9208	18494	647324
22:	07	876	6391	63356	491115
23:	71	243	9572	57897	850604
24:	15	686	7671	58212	280326
25:	44	669	1718	83367	129114
26:	76	858	7809	63607	726978
27:	16	169	5017	18876	291029
28:	12	873	5551	48800	753350
29:	34	413	1040	01683	796684
30:	32	562	0708	98361	927780

DECEMBER	2-DIGIT	3-DIGIT	4-DIGIT	5-DIGIT	6-DIGIT
1:	49	658	6391	64982	866278
2:	78	837	5620	66303	641032
3:	23	570	8537	31230	487369
4:	09	486	5532	13982	437834
5:	79	088	6968	85184	556344
6:	82	851	7903	16870	552009
7:	05	465	3606	00871	852478
8:	16	469	0300	95289	268415
9:	38	525	7358	11035	182449
10:	27	867	9058	01305	919579
11:	88	945	8988	50552	394501
12:	70	940	8355	88507	425248
13:	10	476	0206	52026	548852
14:	49	335	8769	29040	621000
15:	23	270	3255	65363	509983
16:	84	833	3725	51747	903267
17:	86	634	0005	85562	433449
18:	27	361	8568	54131	979819
19:	29	356	3656	75022	358166
20:	56	954	3336	98299	881977
21:	32	455	7821	56956	587763
22:	91	448	8668	70190	715092
23:	43	302	8235	48797	282860
24:	95	079	1743	59904	303576
25:	35	472	8675	47792	842423
26:	26	860	0074	57642	308569
27:	90	077	5826	42773	601520
28:	05	067	5344	65673	189367
29:	89	301	5212	89204	107157
30:	69	834	3525	04824	321101
31:	00	940	4999	20946	816129